Swedish Death Cleaning

Declutter the Stuff of your Life with Döstädning

for a Joyful, Mindful Living

Frederick Rostolno

3 AMAZING BONUS FOR YOU TO DOWNLOAD

when purchasing this book:

BONUS 1

Printable Tracker Sheets

for a 30-day challenge! Our Daily Tracker is designed to be intuitive, making it simple to chart your progress or jot down your thoughts

BONUS 2

Interactive Workbook Pro!

With guided prompts and reflective questions, navigate emotional attachments and celebrate your progress towards mindful living.

BONUS 3 Legacy Letters Guide

Crafting your Personal Legacy with ease. Customizable templates and reflecting exercises including customizable templates

Scroll to the end of Chapter 10 of this book to scan the QR CODE and download your bonuses

Table of Contents

This page was intentionally left blank

Introduction

In the serene countryside of Sweden, there is a special cultural practice that has been handed down through the generations and weaves together a profound understanding of life, death, and our relationship to the material world. This practice, known as "Döstädning," or "Swedish Death Cleaning," invites people, particularly those in their later years of life, to declutter and simplify their surroundings. However, its implications cut across age and cultural divides and offer life lessons that anyone, regardless of background or age, can apply to their own lives.

Swedish Death Cleaning involves more than just getting rid of clutter and organizing one's belongings. At its heart, it is an intimate journey of reflection, letting go, and rediscovering the essence of what truly matters. By embracing Döstädning, we not only prepare our surroundings for life's unexpected events, but we also create a space that brings peace, joy, and mindfulness to our daily lives.

In this book, we will look at the history of Swedish Death Cleaning in Sweden as well as how it can be used in today's chaotic and rapidly changing world.

Whether you are looking for a way to simplify your environment, seeking a deeper connection with the objects that surround you, or wanting to leave a thoughtful legacy for your loved ones, this guide offers insights, strategies, and helpful advice to make your decluttering journey both meaningful and fruitful.

As you explore Swedish Death Cleaning, you'll discover that it is more than just organizing; it is also a celebration of life, a reflection on our transient nature, and a kind gesture of kindness towards those we leave behind.

Let's begin on this journey together, holding hands, as we learn to embrace a life of joyous, conscious living and unearth the beauty and wisdom of Döstädning.

Chapter 1. Swedish Death Cleaning

1.1. What is "Döstädning"

Sweden, a country renowned for its tranquil atmosphere and preference for simplicity, with its gently rolling hills and serene lakes, gave rise to a practice with roots in an awareness of one's own death and the transitory nature of our belongings. This practise is known as "Döstädning," a combination of the Swedish terms "dö" (for death) and "städning" (for cleanliness). Despite the fact that "death cleaning" is the precise translation, it's important to understand that Döstädning encompasses much more than this.

Döstädning is the process of consciously organizing, downsizing and clearing one's belongings in anticipation of one's eventual passing. It's also a highly personal journey into understanding oneself, considering the memories associated with objects, and deciding what actually holds significance in our lives. But it's not only about making things easier for loved ones left behind.

Some people may find the idea unpleasant at first, particularly those unfamiliar with Swedish culture or the philosophy underlying the practice. Döstädning, however, is actually a celebration of life. It's about appreciating the temporary nature of our life and living in the moment by surrounding ourselves with only those things that truly enrich and bring us joy.

Döstädning frequently starts around retirement age in traditional Swedish households. It is regarded as a rite of passage, a period of reflection on one's life journey, and a time to choose which material possessions to keep and which to part with. Döstädning's beauty, though, is that its ideas can be used at any stage of life.

The procedure doesn't just concentrate on throwing away or giving things. Instead, it emphasizes the value of returning to old memories, telling stories, and occasionally even laughing at old mistakes connected with certain objects. Each thing is held, considered, and either maintained with a newfound feeling of purpose or parted with in a thoughtful and usually ceremonial manner.

Imagine having a collection of letters from a childhood friend or the clothes you wore on your first date in your hands. These things are reservoirs of memories, not just objects. Döstädning enables people to take one final deep breath into these memories, savor them, and then choose. Is it time to let them go and pass them on to someone who could find joy or utility in them, or do they still serve a purpose in your life?

Döstädning is essentially about decluttering for a fuller, more thoughtful existence rather than cleaning for death. By the time the process is complete, practitioners frequently discover that they are only surrounded by things that really matter, giving them a clearer physical space and, more importantly, a clearer mind and heart.

You will learn more about Döstädning as we progress through the book and see how it may enlighten our contemporary society by pointing us toward a life of simplicity, intentionality, and profound connection with the past, present, and future.

1.2.   How it differs from other decluttering methods

The desire to simplify our lives has grown stronger globally in recent years. Numerous philosophies urge us to consider our possessions and our relationships with them, from the minimalist movements to the well-known KonMari™ approach championed by Marie Kondo. Döstädning, however, stands out due to its strategy and fundamental philosophy. The end goal of decluttering is the same for all approaches, but Döstädning gives a distinct path and purpose.

1. Rooted in Mortality

Döstädning begins with a recognition of our mortality. This gives the practice an unrivaled depth even though it may look gloomy. By reflecting on the impermanence of life, we declutter not merely for the sake of cleanliness or to achieve a passing aesthetic but also to make the trip easier for ourselves and our loved ones and to truly appreciate the moment.

2. Emphasis on Memory and Legacy

The questions "Does this spark joy?" and "Is this functional?" are frequently used in other decluttering techniques. Döstädning, while considering joy and utility, delves deeper into memory and legacy. It respects the narrative behind every object, understanding that some items carry stories, lessons, and reflections that transcend their material value.

3. Holistic Approach

While many decluttering techniques only address the physical act, Döstädning takes into account both the internal and external environments. A peaceful mind is equally important to having a clean home. The method encourages reflection, encouraging practitioners to think about their possessions, prior experiences, relationships, and personal growth.

4. Respecting the Emotional Journey

Döstädning knows that organizing is more than just a physical activity; it's also emotional. Sometimes, letting go might be accompanied by loss, longing, or guilt. Döstädning advises people to acknowledge these feelings, sit with them, think about them, and then decide. There is no haste, no rigid restrictions, just a gentle, respectful pace that works for each person.

5. Preparation for the Inevitable

Unlike other strategies that could be used to produce a minimalist aesthetic or to make daily living more bearable, Döstädning has the additional layer of planning for end of life. The goal is to ensure our passing doesn't cause our loved ones any more hardship than it already will. We give them one less thing to worry about in their time of loss by taking responsibility for our possessions.

6. Cultural Nuances

Döstädning is deeply rooted in Swedish society and embodies the principles of "lagom" (balance) and moderation. Finding a balance compatible with one's unique life and ideals is important, not practicing extreme minimalism.

To sum up, there are many ways to declutter and legitimate ideologies around it, but Döstädning offers a contemplative and comprehensive journey. It involves more than just clearing up; it involves planning, thinking back, and cherishing. You'll learn about the many advantages of this practice as we continue to study it, and you might find that it resonates with your desire to live an intentional and clear life.

1.3.   Historical and cultural ties in Sweden

In Sweden's vast, captivating landscapes, where the northern lights dance and traditions run deep, a distinct cultural practice has garnered international attention: Döstädning or Swedish Death Cleaning. The core of Döstädning is profoundly connected with the values and history of Sweden.

For centuries, the Swedes have built homes and led lives that are centered on readiness, efficiency, and simplicity to adapt to their environment of harsh winters and short days. To ensure survival and comfort in the harsh Nordic climate, every item in a home had to justify its presence.

The Swedish notion of 'lagom,' which means 'just the right amount,' is key to this mindset. It is a commitment to maintain balance, neither in excess nor in shortage. This fundamental idea of Swedish life naturally extends to Döstädning, guiding people to keep items of actual value—whether functional or emotional—while graciously discarding the unneeded.

Swedish society has long emphasized community and collective well-being. Communities have historically relied on one another to prosper in the face of cold and isolation. This community's attitude influences the practice of Döstädning. It's not just a personal endeavor but also a kind gesture towards loved ones, ensuring that one's passing does not impose an undue burden.

Whereas the end of life is a touchy subject in many cultures, Swedes treat it with a refreshing openness and practicality. This open discussion of life's impermanence permits practices like Döstädning to emerge without the shadow of morbidity. It's a practical step based on consideration and planning.

Swedish folktales, filled with spirits, nature, and profound life teachings, frequently emphasize the transience of life and the desire to leave a lasting, meaningful legacy. Döstädning can be viewed as a tangible manifestation of this age-old yearning to build a riveting narrative.

In this modern age, as mass consumption becomes a global challenge, Döstädning also links age-old wisdom and contemporary necessity. It fosters a conscious return to simplicity and purpose, resonating with the past and the present.

To properly appreciate Döstädning, one must immerse oneself in a practice infused with Swedish history, values, and a strong feeling of purpose. It's more than just a method of decluttering; it's a voyage to the core of Swedish culture and a road to deliberate living.

1.4. The harmony between practicality and mindfulness

Swedish Death Cleaning, or "döstädning," is more than just a practical decluttering technique; it's also a deeply conscious practice that connects the worlds of physical locations and emotional tranquility. This balance of practicality and attention distinguishes it from many other cleaning procedures. But how did these two seemingly disparate concepts become so inextricably linked in this Swedish tradition?

Swedes have traditionally prioritized simplicity, functionality, and durability over simple aesthetic appeal or abundance. This mentality can be found in everything from their well-known furniture designs to their societal principles, emphasizing sustainability and conscious consumption. As a result, practicality is profoundly embedded in Swedish society. However, döstädning amplifies this practical method by incorporating a sense of mindful intention.

Mindfulness is the practice of being completely present in the moment and thoroughly aware of one's thoughts, feelings, and surroundings. When used to decluttering, mindfulness elevates the process from a chore to an introspective adventure. Each object one chooses to keep or discard becomes an occasion to reflect on one's life, values, memories, and future hopes.

Individuals sifting through their stuff are considering more than just the physical utility of objects. They also connect with their past, comprehend their present, and influence their future. A piece of clothing is more than just a garment; it could be a memento of a particular day, a past version of oneself, or a dream yet to come true. An old letter is more than just paper; it's a portal to a treasured memory, a time capsule of feelings.

These emotional insights are deeply intertwined with practical decisions regarding what to preserve in döstädning. For example, while one thing may be kept for everyday utility, another item may be kept for the joy, comfort, or contemplation it provides, even if used infrequently. On the other hand, letting rid of possessions is about making a place for new memories, experiences, and growth, not just physical space.

Essentially, the balance of pragmatism and mindfulness in döstädning results in a holistic decluttering experience. It encourages people to shape their settings to represent their true identities while ensuring that their spaces are functional, sustainable, and filled only with goods that offer value to their lives. Swedes have created a tradition that speaks not just to the home but to the heart.

1.5. Contrasting the global clutter culture with Swedish Simplicity

Globalization has blurred the distinctions between countries and cultures in today's world. It brings a pervasive culture of acquisition: the need to possess the newest technology, fashionable clothing, and infinite things that promise fulfillment and satisfaction. The vast shopping centers, never-ending online retail sites, and constant bombardment of advertisements urging us to buy more and more are all examples of this global clutter culture.

On the other hand, the tranquil simplicity expressed in the Swedish culture starkly contrasts this spending background. It encompasses more than just decluttering and minimalism and emphasizes the value of meaningful relationships, contentment, and the beauty of simplicity.

The calm Swedish countryside, where nature is supreme and people appreciate a slower pace of life, contrasts sharply with the bustling streets of major cities worldwide. This is not meant to imply that modernity or the effects of global consumerism are absent from Sweden. But at its foundation, Swedish tradition places a high value on peace, well-being, and a great respect for the natural world.

Swedish culture values simplicity more than just material possessions. It gets deeper, changing how individuals behave, think, and interact with one another. In Sweden, people know that pleasure comes from the quality of experiences, connections, and true moments of contentment rather than from the quantity of possessions.

Lagom, which means "just the right amount," is the idea that best represents this philosophy. Finding a happy medium and maintaining equilibrium is key. Just right, neither too little nor too much. From their design aesthetics to their social programs, and yes, even their method of decluttering, Swedish society is permeated with this idea.

By embracing döstädning, or Swedish death cleaning, we are engaging in a mindset that opposes the frantic consumerism of the world's clutter culture rather than just adopting a means to organize our homes. We discover a path to a life of purpose, mindfulness, and sincere contentment by comprehending and embracing this Swedish simplicity.

Chapter 2. The Many Benefits of Swedish Death Cleaning

The process of decluttering may appear insignificant in the grand scheme of life's complications. But what if this one action had a multiplicative effect, affecting all parts of our existence and offering both immediate and long-term improvements? With its gentle and thoughtful approach, Swedish Death Cleaning does just that. As we begin this chapter, we'll examine the many advantages of incorporating this Swedish custom, from the physical comfort it offers to our living environments to the significant emotional and social benefits. Join us as we reveal how a decluttering strategy might improve quality of life.

2.1. Physical benefits: Easier maintenance, more space, etc.

Swedish Death Cleaning can create a more peaceful and effective living environment in addition to being a letting-go practice. The physical advantages are fundamentally manifested in clear and immediate ways.

First and foremost, a space that has been decluttered is simpler to maintain. Daily tasks like dusting, vacuuming, and arranging go more quickly when there are fewer extra items to tote around. A certain simplicity comes from understanding that everything in your house has a place and that order doesn't need to be disturbed by clutter.

The gift of space is another. Reclaiming space from extraneous objects is analogous to finding pockets of freedom in the modern world when urban living frequently requires sacrificing square footage. Better movement, the potential for redesign or redecoration, or even simply the pure joy of a more open and airy environment are all made possible by this newly obtained space. Beyond the obvious feeling of space, decluttering can make a home safer. Accident risks in the home are reduced by the absence of obstructions to exits or potential trip hazards. Additionally, a better-organised room is less likely to collect dust and allergies, fostering a healthier living environment.

Finally, a less congested environment uses less energy. Since airflow is improved, the demand for constant heating or cooling may be reduced with fewer obstructions. Similarly, there might be less need for artificial lighting during the day if there were fewer objects to block off natural light.

In summary, Swedish Death Cleaning has significant yet simple bodily advantages. Making space for the pleasures of simplicity and the palpable comfort that comes with it is important, not only in our homes but also in our daily lives.

2.2. Emotional benefits: Less stress, increased happiness, etc.

Accepting Swedish Death Cleaning has effects that extend beyond the physical world and profoundly impact our emotional and psychological health. Having a place to retreat free from chaos is essential in a world full of external influences.

Some of the aspects that relate to the emotional advantages of decluttering include:

1. **The Psychological Impact of Clutter**

At the heart of Swedish Death Cleaning lies an understanding of the emotional weight that possessions can carry. Our accumulated items transform over time into more than simply tangible things; they also become repositories of thoughts, memories, and occasionally even regrets. We unwittingly carry more emotional baggage as our area gets more congested. This mess is a persistent, unobtrusive reminder of things left undone, goals unattained, or painful memories.

2. **Freedom from Emotional Baggage**

Swedish Death Cleaning is more than just throwing things away; it's about breaking free of the emotional bonds to which these things can bind you. Individuals embark on an emotional journey where they review old experiences, deal with residual feelings, and ultimately find closure by actively choosing what to keep and let go.

3. **Creating Space for New Memories**

You may create a space where fresh memories can develop by eliminating things that don't bring you joy or serve a purpose. More than being aesthetically beautiful, a decluttered environment is emotionally liberating. It offers a serenity and clarity frequently suppressed by busy surroundings.

4. **Strengthened Relationships**

Many people discover that döstädning also has a favorable effect on their interpersonal connections. Deeper relationships and respect can be fostered by discussing the meaning of keepsakes, exchanging tales about certain things, or even cooperating when decluttering. The mutual act of letting go can open up lines of communication and foster closer bonds.

5. **Overall Emotional Well-being**

The act of decluttering, especially when done mindfully in the Swedish Death Cleaning style, significantly impacts one's emotional health. It promotes reflection, brings resolution, and creates a greater sense of calm and contentment. People can achieve a more peaceful living free from the weight of superfluous goods by addressing physical and emotional clutter.

2.3. Social benefits: Easier for loved ones in case of sudden demise.

This cleansing technique has a broad societal dimension that frequently goes unnoticed initially yet is extremely intimate. The act of clearing out clutter, sorting through belongings, and letting go benefits not only the person doing it but also everyone around them, especially family and close friends.

Easing the Transition for Loved Ones: The desire to save loved ones from the difficult work of sorting through a lifetime of things is one of the main motivations behind döstädning. Individuals who undertake this work proactively guarantee that the burden of their passing is not too great for those left behind. This loving and thoughtful gesture reduces the likelihood of tension and uncertainty at a time when emotional difficulty is already present.

Many people find comfort in leaving behind a clean, organized space. It provides a sense of finality and a clear, last-minute act of kindness, ensuring that memories are kept and treasured rather than lost in chaos.

Facilitating Meaningful Conversations: The act of decluttering prompts contemplation on the past and the stories and memories connected to certain objects. Sharing these stories with loved ones or friends can lead to enlightening, emotional, and frequently cathartic conversations. It provides an opportunity for intergenerational communication, the transmission of historical accounts, and deepening understanding and appreciation.

Promoting Sustainable Living: Positive social effects result from choosing to recycle, give, or gift objects instead of simply throwing them away. While recycling or upcycling products can lessen their environmental impact, donating items can help those in need. This deliberate decision encourages a sustainability-oriented culture and the welfare of the community.

Thus, Swedish Death Cleaning goes beyond just one's health. It creates a web of interrelated advantages that affect the lives of friends, family, and the larger community. When viewed this way, decluttering is seen as a social activity promoting empathy, understanding, and sustainable living.

Chapter 3. The Joy of Minimalism

The appeal of minimalism increases as our lives fill up with digital distractions and the world with more and more physical stuff. This chapter explores the great freedom and joy that simplicity offers. Swedish Death Cleaning emphasizes decluttering, but minimalism is the guiding principle that encourages a life free of excess and more in sync with what matters most. We'll examine how adopting minimalism may be a life-changing experience that frees us from consumerism's restrictions and enables us to live a life full of experiences, relationships, and purpose.

3.1.   The liberating power of having less

The idea of owning fewer possessions may seem contradictory in our ever-growing consumerist culture. But having fewer possessions brings with it an obvious liberation. The constraints of possession frequently burden our minds, houses, and schedules. It seems weight is lifted off your shoulders when you pare down your possessions to only what is meaningful and necessary.

Acquiring possessions is not inherently negative. It's the accumulation of unnecessary items, often driven by external pressures or fleeting desires, that can become problematic. Imagine residing in a home where every item you own has a useful function or provides you true delight. Such a beautiful area exudes peace and utility. There is no time lost looking for lost belongings, no frustration over messy spaces, and no arduous weekend cleaning chores. Instead, you can find what you need right away, and your surroundings constantly reinforce your sense of calm and order.

This focus on simplicity does not include deprivation; it involves reassessing what is most important. It's a strategy for valuing relationships over transient pleasures, experiences over things, and long-term happiness over transitory pleasures. Adopting a lifestyle with fewer belongings enables one to concentrate more clearly on personal development, spend more time with loved ones, and develop a deeper appreciation for life's simple pleasures. We'll explore the transforming power of minimalism and its profound effects on daily life in greater detail on this journey.

3.2. Breaking free from the consumerist cycle

Modern society often equates consumption with success and happiness. This equation is perpetuated by a barrage of advertisements, promising that the next purchase will bring fulfillment, elevate status, or fill an emotional void. As a result, many people get caught up in a never-ending cycle of consumerism where they buy, accumulate, want more, and then buy again. However, the joy of purchasing a new item frequently wears off fast and is rapidly replaced by the allure of yet another "must-have" item.

This constant need for approval from others and fulfillment might damage one's feeling of self-worth and purpose. The goalposts on this desire treadmill are always moving just out of grasp. This consumerism-centered worldview also has negative emotional and environmental effects. Our purchasing habits should be a key area of contemplation because the production, transportation, and disposal of items substantially impact the environment.

Döstädning encourages pausing, letting people take a step back and critically assess their consumption patterns. It is possible to promote a healthier relationship with goods by comprehending the factors influencing our purchasing decisions and realizing the transient nature of worldly pleasure.

Living without comforts and pleasures is not required when one intentionally realigns one's principles and leaves the consumerist race. It advocates deliberate consumerism or choosing objects based on need, worth, and long-term importance instead of passing fancy or peer pressure. This attitude change might result in a richer life experience when material possessions enhance rather than define the path of life. It involves a dedication to being sincere, thoughtful, and aware that true contentment comes from within rather than off-store shelves.

Chapter 4. The Mindfulness Connection

A deeper journey of mindfulness unfolds within us as we go across the terrain of our homes, organizing and decluttering. Cleaning goes far beyond the material world, especially with the wisdom of döstädning. It becomes a form of meditation, a routine that brings us closer to the present, our feelings, and life itself. We will examine how decluttering and mindfulness are interwoven in this chapter, examining how letting go can result in greater awareness, significant psychological changes, and a more peaceful living. We'll explore the spiritual aspects of cleaning through the Swedish Death Cleaning perspective and learn how decluttering may develop into a healing meditation practice.

4.1.   How decluttering relates to mindfulness.

Decluttering is a spiritual practice as much as a physical one. It necessitates a journey into the recesses of our minds to sort through the emotions, memories, and ties to our stuff. The fundamental ideas of mindfulness, a practice that calls for us to be fully present, attentive, and non-judgmental in every moment, are reflected in this journey.

When practicing traditional mindfulness meditation, the practitioner concentrates on a single object, such as their breath, noticing thoughts and feelings as they come to mind, acknowledging them, and then letting them go. The act of decluttering is strikingly comparable to döstädning. We direct our attention to an object, notice the feelings and memories it brings up, and then, grounded in the present, choose whether to keep it or let it go.

Additionally, as we purge our homes of clutter, we become acutely aware of our spending patterns, emotional ties, and the fleeting nature of material possessions. This knowledge encourages appreciation for what we have and clarity around what matters most in life. By calling our attention to the transience of objects and the enduring value of experiences and relationships, it assists us in differentiating between need and want.
Instead of repressing or eluding our feelings, mindful decluttering encourages us to face and embrace them. This can result in profound insights about who we are and how we interact with the physical environment. In essence, the process turns our homes into havens of intentionality, clarity, and quiet reflecting the inner calm that results from mindfulness practices.

4.2.   The psychology of letting go.

Many spiritual and philosophical traditions strongly emphasize letting go, and for good reason. Letting go—of material belongings, emotions, or past traumas—is fundamental to our psychological health. But why is letting go so difficult for so many of us, and how does that relate to the döstädning principles?

Our attachment to our stuff is rooted in a complicated web of memories and feelings. The things we own frequently act as physical reminders of our past: a keepsake from a treasured vacation, a present from a loved one, or even things we bought during key moments in our lives. These things end up serving as symbols for our identities, goals, and experiences, as well as certain historical moments.

This connection between self-identity and objects makes the decluttering process intensely personal and emotional. Sometimes, letting go can seem like erasing some of our past or admitting that certain hopes or objectives have altered or will never come true. Such realizations can elicit emotions of sadness, regret, or even grief.

But letting go can also feel incredibly liberating. We create room for new experiences, memories, and growth by intentionally deciding letting go of things that no longer serve our current selves. We also reassert our identity's autonomy, reminding ourselves that our actions, ideals, and the relationships we form define us rather than just our things or history.

Döstädning is, therefore, a journey of self-discovery and development that involves more than just clearing up physical space. It presents us with a rare chance to confront our attachments, comprehend their causes, and, with compassion and mindfulness, pick a course that is consistent with our present values and future vision.

4.3. Being present during the cleaning process and the benefits it offers.

When we think of cleaning, our minds often race towards the end goal: a decluttered space. We may approach the task as something to rush through, eager to see the final, tidy result. But döstädning invites us to slow down and immerse ourselves in the moment. It encourages us to touch each item, to recall the memories and emotions they evoke, and to make conscious decisions about their place in our lives.

Being fully present during the cleaning process offers several benefits:

1. **Increased Self-Awareness:** Reflecting on each thing and our attachment to it gives us a deeper understanding of our values, goals, and prior experiences. We start to notice trends in our actions and consumption, which promotes development and change.

2. **Release of emotions:** When we let go of things, we also release the feelings associated with them. This can be a therapeutic experience, especially if you get rid of things that are connected to difficult or unpleasant experiences.

3. **Strengthened Decision-Making:** Consistently deciding what to keep and discard helps us become more adept at making decisions in all aspects of life, not just while decluttering.

4. **Greater Appreciation:** Being present entails truly appreciating the things we decide to maintain. These things are relevant because they accurately portray who we are right now.

5. **Mindful Consumption:** Mindful decluttering practices frequently result in greater consumption with mindfulness. Being present during döstädning teaches us to be more selective with what we bring into our environment, ensuring they all serve a useful function.

By merging mindfulness and döstädning, we transform the procedure from a task to a transformative experience. We not only improve the atmosphere, but we also develop a stronger bond with our memories and aspirations.

Chapter 5. Preparing for Your Decluttering Journey

Swedish Death Cleaning is a journey that involves thorough organization and the right equipment to achieve a transforming experience. It is similar to preparing for an instructive pilgrimage. It's critical to prepare yourself emotionally and physically for the difficulties and realizations you're about to encounter before jumping deeply into decluttering. This chapter serves as a road map, highlighting the best mindset to adopt and the tools to gather to organize your space and spirit. Knowing where to start and what to anticipate can be crucial to the success of any big journey. Let's prepare you for a liberating and enriching decluttering journey.

5.1. Embracing the right mindset for effective decluttering

Our mental environments frequently reflect our actual surroundings. A messy home can lead to a cluttered mind, and the reverse is also true. To maximize the advantages of decluttering, it is crucial to align our ideas and emotions before beginning the Swedish Death Cleaning procedure.

The first step is realizing that decluttering isn't merely a task but also a way to live a more deliberate and intentional life. The following are important mindsets to cultivate:

Acceptance: Recognise and accept the fact that you have accumulated stuff throughout the years, some of which may not have any further utility for you. Accepting this reality, you can approach decluttering without feeling guilty or regret.

Intention: Decluttering should be done with a purpose in mind. Having a clear objective can act as a driving force, whether it's to make more space, relieve tension, or leave behind a legacy free of unwanted burdens for loved ones.

Mindfulness: Through the process, stay present. When you come across an old picture or object, memories often start to flood back. Allow yourself the space to reflect while keeping your decluttering goals in mind.

Gratitude: Consider this procedure an opportunity to appreciate the value each object brought into your life at some point rather than just seeing it as something to eliminate. This perspective improves the experience and intensifies the sensation of accomplishment.

Letting Go: Recognise that by letting go of things, you're making room for new chances, memories, and experiences. Embrace the ability to let go, understanding that doing so can lead to the development of new beginnings.

It's also important to address any emotions that surface, including joy, sorrow, nostalgia, or even anxiety. These emotions are essential to the procedure, making the journey intimate and transforming. Swedish Death Cleaning, when done with the appropriate attitude, can be as healing for the soul as it is for your home.

5.2.   Assembling your toolkit: what you'll need

It's essential to have the proper equipment available before starting a decluttering project. Consider decluttering as an adventure, and just as a climber wouldn't set out without their climbing equipment, you shouldn't do the same. Making your toolkit ensures that you handle things carefully, sort them properly, and make deliberate decisions, in addition to making the process more efficient.

Basic Supplies: At the very heart of decluttering are the basic supplies. These typically include:

Durable Boxes and Bags: Ensure you have enough strong boxes and bags before starting decluttering. These will be essential for categorizing items to keep, donate, recycle, or discard.

Notepad or Journal: You can discover goods as you sort through things you wish to learn more about, sell, or give to particular people. To ensure that these ideas don't get lost in the chaos of decluttering, a notepad can be a priceless tool.

Markers and Labels: You can instantly determine the contents of any box or bag thanks to clear labeling. This might be extremely helpful when you're sorting and need to keep track of various categories.

Trash Bags: There will be items you'll immediately recognize as trash. Having trash bags on hand makes it easier to discard them promptly.

Tape Measure: A tape measure can be really helpful if you're thinking about organizing your space or purchasing new storage options to make sure everything fits precisely.

Gloves: Some things can be covered in dust, be rusted, or have aged poorly. Your hands will be protected, and the cleaning process will be more hygienic if you use gloves.

Cleaning Supplies: Stock up on some basic cleaning supplies. Before putting things back or reorganizing, now is a great time to briefly clean spaces.

Recycling Guide: There are different recycling regulations in each region. Having a disposal guide on hand ensures you dispose of things properly and per environmental best practices.

For Valuable or Fragile Items:

Bubble Wrap & Tissue Paper: If you discover items you wish to donate or sell, especially if they're fragile, having protective materials ensures they remain in good shape.

Digital Camera or Smartphone: Taking pictures of items you're unsure about getting rid of, especially ones with sentimental value, might help you preserve memories without keeping the physical object.

For Paperwork or Documents:

File Folders: Perfect for classifying and preserving any critical documents you desire to save.

Labels: Label file folders with descriptive names, such as "Tax Returns," "Medical Records," "Warranties," etc., to make them easy to find.

Accordion File Organizer: Useful for storing various document types separated but together in a portable container

Binders: For records, such as certificates or licenses, that may need to be regularly accessed or presented in a more formal manner.

Digital Decluttering:

External Hard Drive or Cloud Storage: Having extra storage to back up vital files before you start cleaning your devices can be crucial if part of your decluttering involves digital environments.

Scanner or Scanning App: Digitalize important documents to reduce physical clutter. This is ideal for items you want to retain but not necessarily in paper form.

Always keep in mind that building a toolbox is more about utilizing what you currently have and just buying what is absolutely essential. It's an enabler that helps you transform, ensures you treat your stuff with respect, and makes the decluttering process go more easily.

5.3.   Setting clear, actionable goals

Any worthwhile endeavor starts with setting goals, and decluttering is no exception. A foundation for direction, action, and dedication may be built with the help of a clear vision. By establishing specific objectives for your decluttering procedure, you may create a roadmap that reveals the way ahead and makes the journey less difficult and more strategic.

Imagine the intended result before you even start. What do you hope to achieve with this journey? Perhaps you aim to create a peaceful living environment, reduce stress, or simply make daily routines smoother by eliminating the excess. Whatever the incentive, it must be compelling since this emotional connection will keep you motivated throughout the procedure.

Then, be specific about your objectives. Set more specific objectives, such as "declutter the house," rather than a general one. Think of phrases like "Clean out the attic by the end of the month" or "Sort through all the books in the living room by Friday." By breaking the task into smaller, time-bound pieces, you can ensure each objective is doable.

Another successful strategy is to connect your decluttering objectives to events or milestones, for instance, before a special occasion or before a big life transition like a move or the addition of a family member. These occasions can serve as natural deadlines, giving your decluttering project urgency and direction. Regular goal evaluation and modification are also advantageous. Because of the ebb and flow of life, our plans frequently need to be flexible. Consider further breaking down a goal if you find it too difficult. Conversely, you might want to give yourself a little more challenge if you finish tasks faster than expected.

Finally, be proud of all your accomplishments, no matter how minor. You will get closer to your ideal space with every drawer you organize, an empty shelf, and every box you give. By recognizing and celebrating these milestones, you may sustain motivation and build a sense of pride and success in your decluttering journey.

Chapter 6. The Swedish Death Cleaning Process

Starting this journey is like setting sail on the peaceful waters of contemplation, with waves of nostalgia and emotional realizations. However, success on any journey depends on knowing what lies ahead. In this chapter, we go in-depth into the Döstädning process and walk you through each careful step. We'll arm you with the knowledge and awareness needed to traverse this illuminating experience with confidence and purpose, from the initial evaluation of your stuff through the organization of the items you decide to preserve. With the wind of Swedish knowledge at your back, you'll be prepared to set sail toward a clutter-free and peaceful living space.

6.1. Beginning with Assessment

Any decluttering journey should start with the crucial act of assessment. It's similar to snapping a photo of one's surroundings to fully comprehend how they are right now. The remaining stages of the process are guided by this initial step as a compass. This section will examine how to identify the areas and categories that require attention, how to effectively manage your time, and the significance of adopting a methodical approach. Doing a thorough assessment may create a clear vision that will ensure the Döstädning method's subsequent phases proceed precisely and with purpose.

6.1.1. Identifying and listing areas and categories to tackle

It's essential to identify and list the places and categories in your home that are strong candidates for decluttering during the earliest assessment phases. This decluttering method method strongly emphasizes precision rather than approaching the process with a broad, sweeping lens. Making a thorough list of any areas that jump out as untidy or disorganized should be your first step as you stroll through each room of your house.

For instance, kitchens may include excessive cookware, gadgets, and utensils, some of which may be decades old. Similar to this, closets may overflow with clothing that does not fit or complement one's style. Not to mention the attics, basements, and garages are frequently the final resting places for things we've outgrown but haven't yet gotten rid of.

Categorization is key following a visual survey. Describe the space in more detail than just writing "bedroom" or "living room," such as "bedroom - under the bed," "bedroom - top shelf of the closet," "living room - DVD collection," and so on. The rigorous categorization makes the process more manageable, which also ensures that no object, no matter how small or hidden, is missed. This methodical, thorough technique ensures that every item is examined and every place is revitalized, which prepares the ground for efficient decluttering.

6.1.2. Estimating the time required

One of the most important steps in the Swedish Death Cleaning procedure is determining how long the decluttering will take. It guarantees that you set aside enough time to give each area the focus it need, without feeling rushed or overextended. This estimate covers the time required for reflection, decision-making, and emotional processing in addition to the physical act of decluttering.

When estimating time, consider the following:

Size and Density of the Area: A little bathroom drawer might only take thirty minutes, whereas a crowded attic might take all day or a weekend.

Emotional Weight: Many memories are associated with certain things or places. It could take longer to go through old photo albums or personal letters because of the feelings and memories they arouse.

Decision-making Process: Do you have a speedy decision-making process or require time to think things through? Identify your decision-making style and consider it.

Physical Effort: Moving large objects into a room or thoroughly cleaning them could take longer or perhaps require breaks.

If your initial estimate isn't exact, that's okay. Starting is the key. You can always change your timetable if you realize that you miscalculated. Keep in mind that it's not a race. Being thorough and mindful is the goal. Always give yourself wiggle room for any unforeseen feelings or difficulties. As much as the process is about the finished product of a decluttered environment, it's also about the journey and what you discover about yourself along the way.

6.2. Sorting & Categorizing Items

A cornerstone of the Swedish Death Cleaning procedure is sorting and categorizing things. Even though the task might appear overwhelming initially, breaking it down into doable pieces can make it effective and therapeutic. The goals are to find a rational framework that works for you and bring order to the chaos.

Gathering all related items from different areas of your home into one place is the first step. No matter where they are currently kept, this entails gathering every book, article of clothing, or kitchen tool. By seeing everything you own in a specific category together, you can more easily determine what's essential and what's redundant. Consider your objects' main duties or functions after that. For instance, You might have business, casual, fitness, and apparel for special occasions in your wardrobe. Your initial categories can be based on these.

Delve further after you have grouped comparable objects. In each group, evaluate each item. Do they overlap each other? What items have you not used in a long time? Exist any items that don't match your personal style or way of living right now? The things that truly value your life and those just taking up space can be distinguished through introspection. Use the "memory, utility, and necessity" framework described below. An item may have sentimental value (memory), be useful (utility), or be necessary for day-to-day living (necessity). Although not all items will neatly fit into these categories, they offer a framework for seeing and assessing your assets.

Try to be patient with yourself as you sort yourself into these categories. Recognize that it's normal to have a connection to things, even if you don't use them or need them anymore. But by classifying and organizing, you're drawing a road map to a more ordered, useful living environment, and each choice moves you a step closer to that objective.

6.2.1. Using the "memory, utility, necessity" framework

The "memory, utility, necessity" approach gives the decluttering process complexity and nuance. It explores our relationships with our belongings on an emotional and practical level, going beyond just how useful they are.

Memory: This group of things has sentimental value. They might be souvenirs from travels, presents from loved ones, or things connected to important life events. Although they might not be useful daily, their emotional importance cannot be denied. But it's important to assess these things critically. Is it beneficial to your current well-being to cling to anything from the past, or does it just clog your home and mind? Instead of getting rid of every memento-filled object, the objective is to build a collection that truly reflects who you are right now.

Utility: These are the workhorses of our daily operations. The tools at our workspace or the culinary equipment we use for cooking all have a certain function. Consider this question while assessing an item's utility: Is it functional? Is it in decent shape? Do I have numerous products that are used for the same thing? By simplifying these necessities, we can ensure that what is left is effective and efficient in fulfilling its function.

Necessity: These things are indispensable. They are items that we cannot live without, such as particular prescriptions, significant papers, or everyday apparel. When sorting items based on necessity, it's vital to distinguish between what feels like a necessity and what truly is one. For instance, although having a large collection of shoes may seem required, you may just need a few pairs you use frequently.

Understanding and implementing the "memory, utility, necessity" concept provides you with a varied tool. It's a compass that helps you make informed decisions about what to keep and what to let go of, ensuring that your living space reflects your requirements, values, and objectives.

6.3.   Deciding What to Keep

Making decisions on what to keep and discard might not be so easy sometimes. The value we place on items often exceeds their monetary value; they hold memories, feelings, and stories from our past. This emotional connection, though, can make the decluttering process feel burdensome or even paralyzing. In this chapter, we will look at tactics and standards for evaluating items through emotional and functional lenses, ensuring that the items you keep correspond with your present requirements and future goals. By the conclusion, you can make informed decisions that honor your past while paving the way for a brighter future.

6.3.1.   Evaluating items through emotional and functional lenses

Navigating our belongings demands more than a superficial examination. To fully declutter, we must assess items from two perspectives: emotional significance and functional utility.

Emotional Evaluation:

Narrative & Sentiment: Some items tell a story. Perhaps it's a souvenir from a memorable trip or a gift from a dear friend. While these items might not hold much functional value, their sentimental worth can be immeasurable. When assessing such items, ask yourself: Does this object still resonate with my current emotional state? Does it bring joy, or has its narrative run its course?

Transitional Objects: We frequently save items that have helped us through difficult times. These transitional objects may have brought solace during times of grief, transition, or personal turmoil. However, our emotional reliance on these objects may lessen as we mature and recover. It is critical to recognize when it is time to let go so that past traumas or challenges do not bind us.

Legacy & Heirlooms: Objects passed down over generations can carry a sense of obligation. Consider discussing with family members, recognizing their emotional importance, and assessing how they fit into the larger family story before retaining or letting go.

Functional Evaluation:

Utility & Frequency: The most basic question is, "Do I use this?" Even if an item is in perfect state, its functional worth is doubtful if it has been collecting dust. Consider how often you use it and whether it fits your everyday routine.

Condition & Durability:

Duplication: We frequently accumulate multiple versions of the same item. Duplicated items, whether they are culinary gadgets, tools, or clothing, can add to the clutter. Choose the version that best serves you, and consider discarding the others.

Space & Aesthetics: While some items are essential, they may be too huge for our living area or do not match our intended aesthetic. These items, while useful, have the potential to upset the balance of our environment. Consider alternatives or substitutes that are more appropriate for your space and style.

You'll discover your complicated relationships with your stuff as you work your way through the layers of emotional and functional appraisal. This all-encompassing strategy ensures that your decluttered area is functional and strongly resonates with your emotional landscape. Accept this process with patience and introspection, and treasure the revelations and clarity it brings to light.

6.3.2. Recognizing and overcoming emotional barriers

As you work your way through the layers of emotional and functional appraisal, you'll discover the complicated relationships you have with your belongings. This comprehensive technique ensures that your decluttered space is functional and powerfully connects with your emotional landscape. Accept this process with patience and contemplation, and cherish the insights and clarity it provides.

It is common to feel guilty when considering letting go of gifts from loved ones, expensive purchases, or items that hold prior memories. This guilt could stem from perceived waste or a sense of betrayal towards the person who gave the thing. We sometimes keep items out of a sense of obligation. This could be due to societal expectations, family expectations, or personal views. Holding onto inherited items, for example, because it's expected within the family, even if they have little personal importance. Objects can also become entwined with our sense of self. Books we've read, clothes we wear, and hobbies we used to like can all become symbolic representations of who we are. Letting go can feel like letting go of a piece of oneself.

Shifting the perspective can help you handle these feelings. Instead of dwelling on the loss, consider the advantages of decluttering. Recognize the freedom, ease, and clarity that a decluttered environment provides. This change can help to alleviate feelings of remorse and obligation. Discuss your feelings with loved ones, especially when dealing with shared or inherited items. Their perspective may provide new insights, and their assistance may help overcome guilt and obligation. If you're unsure about getting rid of something, put it in a 'maybe' box for a specific period of time, say six months. It may be simpler to let go if you don't find yourself reaching for the object during this time. Consider capturing the spirit of items that have sentimental significance but contribute to clutter through photography, journaling, or digital archiving. By keeping the memory, you can let go of the object without fearing losing your identity. An outsider's perspective can sometimes provide clarity. Consider seeking the assistance of a friend, family member, or professional organizer in your decluttering efforts. Their objective viewpoint can assist in more efficiently navigating emotional boundaries. It is critical to confront these emotional hurdles head-on. This technique is about navigating and purifying the emotional terrain and physical decluttering. As you overcome these obstacles, you will discover a deeper connection with yourself and a greater appreciation for the items you choose to keep.

6.4. Letting Go Gracefully

Not merely the process of decluttering but also how we part with our stuff is one of the most meaningful components of Swedish Death Cleaning. Letting go is an act of grace that incorporates respect, gratitude, and attention. After delving into the complexities of deciding what to keep, we must now focus on the intricate process of releasing items. This entails honoring the memories and sentiments of our possessions while finding sustainable, appropriate, and meaningful methods to release them. Whether donating, recycling, gifting, or even throwing away, the motive behind the act is important. In this chapter, we will discuss the importance of letting go with grace and the different paths we may take to ensure our items find their next purpose or location as we continue our journey towards a decluttered, mindful living.

6.4.1. Respecting memories while releasing items

Our possessions often serve as tangible representations of intangible memories and emotions. The scarf from a loved one, the trinket bought during a memorable trip, the book gifted by a cherished friend; each item may carry a story, a sentiment, or a memory. And this is precisely what makes parting with them challenging. But Swedish Death Cleaning teaches us that while we may release the physical item, the memories remain undisturbed, held securely within our minds and hearts.

When we begin the process of letting go, we must first honor the memories associated with each object. Take a minute to ponder, recall, and be grateful for the part it played in your life. This acknowledgment ensures that the memory is kept even if the item is no longer present.

Our lives, on the other hand, are dynamic and ever-changing. Some items' significance may fade over time, making it simpler to let go. In other cases, the object may no longer be compatible with our current lifestyle, priorities, or available space. When this occurs, we must change our perspective and consider the act of letting go as an opportunity. We are not only making space in our homes by releasing items but also allowing someone else to build new memories and tales with them.

Consider capturing the story or memory linked with the object to make the process more meaningful. Capturing the spirit of the object, whether through a diary entry, an image, or even a digital archive, can make the process of letting go less scary. It acts as a reminder that, while the physical object has vanished, its emotional and historical imprint remains with us, undiminished.

Remember that letting go is not a loss but a development as you go through your decluttering journey. It's about moving away from tangible clutter and embracing and cherishing the rich fabric of memories and events that truly characterize our lives.

6.4.2.   Sustainable ways to discard: recycling, donating, gifting

Decluttering involves more than just discarding items; it also involves giving those items a new purpose, a new life, or, at the very least, an eco-friendly ending. Swedish Death Cleaning focuses on cleaning our spaces and doing it with mindfulness and sustainability in mind. By approaching decluttering from this perspective, we cultivate a sense of responsibility, ensuring that our activities now do not negatively impact our planet's future.

First and foremost, think about donating items in good shape. Organizations, charities, and shelters may frequently utilise these items, giving them new life and ensuring they serve a purpose. Clothes, toys, cookware, and books—there's nearly always a spot where these items can be valued and enjoyed again. Donating eliminates trash and helps people in need, creating a positive and giving loop.

Consider gifting items that aren't in good enough condition to donate but still have some life in them. Perhaps a family member, acquaintance, or neighbor will find them useful. Gifting can be a meaningful method to pass on items that may no longer carry substantial worth for you but may be extremely valuable to someone else.

However, there will always be items that cannot be donated or gifted. Turn to recycling for these. Recycling protocols differ for diverse materials such as paper, glass, plastics, and metals. Learn about your community's recycling policies and facilities. We limit environmental harm and the pressure on landfills by ensuring that items are properly recycled.

Finally, for items that cannot be recycled, it is critical to dispose of them properly. Avoid contributing to environmental deterioration by hurriedly discarding non-biodegradable items. Instead, look into eco-friendly disposal options that may be available in your area.

We do more than just clear our homes when we use sustainable disposal methods; we also help the environment and society. It's a comprehensive strategy that emphasizes the essence of Swedish Death Cleaning: living with intention and leaving a legacy of caring.

6.5. Organizing and Storing the Retained

We're left with items that have true value and purpose in our lives after carefully decluttering, analyzing, and discarding. These items deserve to be well organized and stored. This isn't just about arranging things nicely; it's about designing processes that assure each item's accessibility, lifespan, and continuous appreciation. In this chapter, we'll look at the art and science of organizing and storing the items you've chosen to save. We'll show you how to honor and showcase your items, ensuring that they suit your living environment and enrich your daily life. We will use inspiration from Swedish homes noted for their perfect organization.

6.5.1. Swedish organizational techniques

After a meticulous process of decluttering, assessing, and discarding, we are left with items that have actual value and purpose in our lives. These items are deserving of proper organization and storage. This isn't just about neatly organizing things; it's about creating routines that ensure each item's accessibility, longevity, and ongoing enjoyment. In this chapter, we'll examine the art and science of organizing and saving the items you've decided to save. Using inspiration from Swedish homes known for their impeccable organizing, we'll teach you how to honor and showcase your items, ensuring that they suit your living space and improve your daily life.

Another principle is to make the most of vertical space. Swedish homes, particularly in cities, are frequently compact. Using vertical space, such as walls, for shelving or hanging storage helps to keep the floor area clear and the room expansive.

Also key is transparency. Whether it's glass-fronted cabinets or clear storage containers, seeing what's inside helps with speedy retrieval and serves as a reminder of what you have, decreasing the possibility of excessive accumulations.

Finally, multi-functionality is a distinguishing feature. Popular furniture and storage solutions serve several functions, such as a bed with drawers underneath or a coffee table that doubles as storage. This ensures that space is efficiently used while keeping the room's visual appeal.

Adopting these Swedish organizational techniques will help you transform your home, making it more efficient, appealing, and in sync with your decluttered lifestyle. Understanding the idea underlying these practices allows you to readily tailor them to your specific needs and home setting.

6.5.2.   Proper storage to preserve and easily access items

When done correctly, storage is more than merely storing items. It's about preserving treasured possessions while still making them accessible. Maintaining a decluttered environment requires striking a balance between preservation and accessibility.

Begin with the storage containers' quality. Choose strong, long-lasting solutions to shield items from dust, humidity, and potential harm. Consider specialized storage solutions for items that are sensitive to light or temperature fluctuations, such as photographs or certain materials.

When determining where to place items, keep the frequency of use in mind. Items used daily or weekly should be kept within arm's reach, while less often used items can be kept on higher shelves or in deeper storage locations. This will eliminate the need for excessive shuffling and searching.

It is critical to store items that require particular care in accordance with their specifications. For example, delicate materials should be stored in permeable cotton bags, while cutlery should be stored in anti-tarnish pouches. Labeling is your friend. A clear, short label, especially for boxes or containers stored away from direct view, can speed up retrieval, saving you from opening many boxes before finding what you need. Seasonal items that are rotated can also save space and minimize clutter. For example, storing winter items throughout the summer and vice versa guarantees you just have the necessities for the current season.

Lastly, remember to revisit your storage spaces periodically. Even with the best intentions, it's natural for spaces to become cluttered or disorganized over time. A regular check, maybe bi-annually, can help in tweaking the storage setup as per current needs and ensuring it remains efficient.

Chapter 7. Daily Routine: Incorporating Swedish Death Cleaning into everyday life

After we've grasped the fundamentals of Döstädning and completed the initial deep cleanse, how do we incorporate this illuminating philosophy into our daily lives? It may appear difficult to go from a one-time decluttering event to a sustainable, regular practice. The beauty of döstädning, however, is in its flexibility to daily life, creating a constantly harmonious living area.

In this chapter, we'll look at how to incorporate Swedish Death Cleaning ideas into our daily lives and we'll delve into tactics that keep our environments decluttered and enhance our daily experiences. The goal is to maintain a relationship with our possessions, ensuring that our living environments stay bright, functional, and truly expressive of who we are.

7.1. Beginning the day with a mindful assessment

Beginning the day with intent sets the tone for the rest of the day. In the framework of Swedish Death Cleaning, this intentionality translates into a morning exercise that includes a brief yet mindful examination of your living space. Take a few peaceful moments to survey your surroundings before the hustle and bustle of the day takes over. Look for any items that may have been misplaced the day before or now seem unneeded.

It's not about doing a comprehensive decluttering session every morning; it's about creating a continual awareness of your surroundings. Maybe you notice a book on your nightstand that you completed but haven't put away or a jacket hanging over a chair that might be hung in the closet. Addressing these minor activities daily ensures that they do not pile up and become overwhelming.

Furthermore, this exercise strengthens the link between your physical environment and your mental state. As you align your space, you also align your ideas, allowing you to enter the day with a clearer mind. This symbiotic relationship between external tidiness and internal clarity is a cornerstone of the döstädning concept, boosting task efficiency and mental peace.

7.2. Daily mini-decluttering sessions: 4-step process

Adopting the Döstädning attitude does not rely solely on huge decluttering activities. Introducing short, daily mini-decluttering exercises can be game changers in making decluttering an embedded part of our everyday lives. These short and concentrated workshops emphasize the habit of decluttering rather than the act itself.

Why Daily Mini-Sessions?

Consistency is the key to everyday mini-sessions. You may not feel like you're making much progress in a 10-minute session, but over the course of a month, that's 300 minutes of concentrated decluttering. The sessions aren't about how much you can get rid of but about doing the act of analyzing and deciding a habit.

First: Identifying Target Areas

Every day, choose a small, specific area or category. It could be:

A drawer at your desk stuffed with random items.

A section of your wardrobe, such as socks or belts.

A kitchen cabinet stocked with spices or canned items.

A portion of your bookshelves.

Second: Setting the Timer

Limit each session to 15 to 20 minutes. This method guarantees that the task remains manageable and does not become overwhelming. You'll be astonished at how much you can get done in this short burst of concentrated attention.

Third: Making Quick Decisions

Because time is of the essence, you must make quick decisions. It is useful to have a specific criterion in mind:

Is this anything I've used in the last year?

Does this provide you joy or serve a purpose?

Is this item still in good shape, or should it be fixed or recycled?

Fourth: Post-Decision Actions

It is critical to act quickly after deciding on an item. This helps prevent the item from ending up in a cluttered space. Here are some options:

→ **Keep**: If you want to keep something, be sure it's in the right place. Can it be better organized? Is there a specific place for it? If not, create one. This ensures that everything has a 'home'.

→ **Donate**: Place items in a designated donation box that are still in good condition but no longer serve you. Take this box to your nearest charity or donation center once it is filled.

→ **Trash**: Some items are beyond repair and are not recyclable. The trash is their last resort. However, always dispose of items responsibly.

→ **Gift**: Sometimes, an item is no longer useful to you, but you know someone who would. Place it in a 'gift box'. Remember to give it to the person the next time you see them.

→ **Repair (optional)**: Items that are damaged but still valuable should be placed in a ' repair box. Set up a weekly or monthly time to repair or transport these items to a specialist.

→ **Sell (optional)**: If an item is valuable and in good condition, it may be worth selling. Platforms like eBay, Craigslist, or local garage sales can be good options.

For an extended explanation see Chapter 8.2

Make the mini-session a habit by scheduling it at a set time of day. It may be your first thing in the morning, a lunchtime break, or a method to unwind in the evening.

Seeing the Cumulative Effect

While each session may appear modest, everyday decluttering has a big cumulative effect. Over the course of several weeks and months, these pockets of decluttered space combine to form a more organized, calm, and productive house. Daily mini-decluttering sessions benefit both your physical and emotional spaces. The act becomes a mindfulness moment in your day when you are fully present. It cultivates an intentionality habit in which you continually review what deserves space in your life.

While the larger sweeps of Swedish Death Cleaning have a transforming force, the persistent, daily mini-sessions ground the philosophy in daily life. Decluttering becomes less of a huge effort and more of a daily act of awareness and intentionality when you set up a few minutes each day, resulting in a house that consistently reflects your beliefs and priorities.

7.3. Evening reflections and preparations for the next day

Taking a minute to pause and think at the conclusion of a day of mindful decluttering and reorganization can be both grounding and revitalizing. Evening reflections allow you to think about what went well during the day, what problems arose, and how to prepare for the next day. This chapter goes into the nightly contemplation routine, highlighting its significance in the Swedish Death Cleaning process.

Evening is a transitional period, a link between the day that has passed and the one that is yet to come. After a day of sorting, discarding, and organizing, you may feel a sense of accomplishment, nostalgia, or even sadness. It is critical to recognise these feelings without judgement, accepting them as natural reactions to the process.

Reflecting on Accomplishments and Challenges: Begin your evening ritual by reviewing what you've managed to organize and declutter. Celebrate your accomplishments, no matter how minor, and acknowledge your efforts. Take note, however, of any areas where you may have struggled. Were there any items that were especially difficult to part with? Or perhaps a space that appeared too large to tackle? By identifying these difficulties, you can psychologically prepare yourself to approach them differently in the future or devote more time to them.

Journaling as a Tool: Consider maintaining a decluttering diary in which you can scribble down your thoughts. Write about the memories linked with the items, the emotions they elicited, and how you felt after letting them go. This written record is a tribute to your journey and can be reviewed for motivation and insight.

Planning for Tomorrow: After you've had some time to contemplate, go on to the next day. Consider the regions or categories you want to focus on. Perhaps you've been avoiding a drawer or a category of items you're eager to sort through. You may approach the next day with clarity and purpose if you set your intentions the night before.

Setting the Stage: Spend a few minutes before going to bed prepping your decluttering space for the next session. This could include arranging boxes or containers, storing tools, or simply making room to work. You'll be more encouraged to dig in the next day if your atmosphere is organized and appealing.

Every Swedish Death Cleaning procedure phase is an opportunity for awareness and insight. Evening reflections and preparations serve as bookends to your decluttering efforts, helping you digest the day's events and anticipate and plan for the next. It's more than a routine; it's a ritual that feeds the soul while cleansing your surroundings.

BE SURE TO DOWNLOAD THE EXTRA BONUSES AT THE END OF CHAPTER 10 FOR MORE TOOLS TO HELP YOU ON YOUR JOURNEY

Chapter 8. Nine Practical Strategies for Efficient Decluttering

Beginning the Swedish Death Cleaning journey requires more than motivation and emotion; it also necessitates a variety of practical tactics that can simplify the process and ensure efficient cleansing. As we explore this transformative strategy, it becomes clear that systematic techniques can streamline our efforts and improve the whole experience. This chapter introduces readers to several decluttering tactics, and each is customized to various decluttering scenarios, ranging from the classification of items to the handling of sentimental belongings. Based on döstädning principles, these tactics ensure that each decluttering session brings you one step closer to living a life of clarity and purpose. Whether you're new to decluttering or searching for a more refined approach, the techniques in this chapter will improve your experience by making it more systematic, efficient, and gratifying.

8.1. Strategy n.1: Tackling Categories, Not Rooms

Decluttering by categories rather than rooms provides a more organized and comprehensive approach. Instead of delving into various places, such as the bedroom or kitchen, you concentrate on specific categories, for example, clothing, books, kitchenware, or sentimental items. This approach provides many advantages. For starters, it provides a unified strategy that ensures all items of a category are addressed collectively. Consider gathering every article of clothes from every part of the house, resulting in consistent conclusions about what to keep and what to toss. It also eliminates redundancy. Once a category is complete, you're less likely to encounter a similar item in another room, lowering the danger of retaining needless duplicates. The category-based method narrows your focus, making the work of decluttering appear less intimidating. Instead of being overwhelmed by the contents of an entire room, your focus is on a specific group of items. This strategy also facilitates a smoother emotional transition. Start with less emotionally charged categories, such as kitchenware, to gain momentum and confidence before getting into more sentimental items. Decluttering by category also aids in optimizing space as you advance. You better understand the storage requirements for each category, resulting in more effective storage solutions and a more organized home. To get the most out of this method, assemble everything in the chosen category, display it prominently, and apply the Döstädning principles to determine what really connects with your life's values.

Finally, a category-focused approach is more organized by definition. Instead of bouncing between rooms or areas, you'll walk through each category individually, making the process more controlled and logical. As you see entire categories decluttered and improved, this order can boost your sense of accomplishment and development.

8.1.1. The 9-step guide for categorizing

Using a category-based approach to decluttering involves a certain level of organization from the start. Here's a step-by-step strategy for making categorizing systematic and effective:

1. **List Out Categories**: Make a comprehensive list of all the categories that apply to your possessions. Common categories include books, clothing, cookware, gadgets, collectibles, and more. You can change

the level of detail in these categories to suit your comfort level, for example, dividing "clothing" into "shirts," "pants," "accessories," etc.

2. **Prioritize**: Not all categories are equally important or labor-intensive. Sort categories according to their emotional resonance or volume. Before going on to more sentimental items like family heirlooms, it could be simpler for some people to start with a less emotive category, like kitchenware.

3. **Allocate Specific Time**: Give each category a set time to fill. By doing this, you can stay on task and avoid feeling overloaded. It can take as little as 30 minutes for minor categories, but for bigger ones, it can take many hours or even days.

4. **Gather All Items**: Pull every relevant item from all corners of your home for each category. You can more accurately assess what is necessary by addressing the vast amount of items in a specific category.

5. **Evaluate**: With the entire category spread out before you begin the evaluation process. Consider each item's usefulness, sentimental value, condition, and importance to your life now and soon.

6. **Sort and Decide**: For items you want to preserve, donate, recycle, and dispose of, designate specific spaces or containers. When sorting, be sincere and rigorous while keeping in mind the fundamentals of Swedish Death Cleaning.

7. **Document**: Documenting your progress can be useful as you travel through the categories. This can be as basic as documenting the process with before-and-after pictures or writing down your thoughts on any emotional or useful insights you may have gained.

8. **Move to the Next**: When a category is finished, put the items you've decided to keep in their designated locations and immediately deal with the rest, whether that means giving, recycling, or discarding. Afterward, proceed to the next category on your list.

9. **Reassess Periodically**: Your relationship with items might change as the months and years go by. It's helpful to frequently review categories to make sure your possessions reflect your ideals and position in life.

8.1.2. The benefits of this approach

Döstädning can be significantly streamlined and improved by adopting a category-based decluttering strategy. When you concentrate on categories, it becomes clear how much of one certain sort of item you already own,

---

which helps you determine your needs more precisely. This increased consciousness might act as a motivator for letting go.

For instance, gathering every book from every room in the house could be revealing when dealing with the category of books. You can discover that you own many copies of a book or series you previously wanted to read but are no longer interested in. The ability to see things from above helps with decision-making. Organizing by category also encourages uniformity. Examining all garments at once guarantees that decisions align with your overall decluttering objectives rather than deciding on one shirt's fate in isolation in the bedroom and another when browsing the laundry room.

Additionally, by using this technique, future accumulation of needless items can be avoided. Future purchases or acquisitions are made with greater mindfulness when you are familiar with every item in a category. Knowing exactly what you already have will make you think twice before adding another item.

A systematic, category-based decluttering plan can bring clarity, keep things moving, and make Swedish Death Cleaning efficient and immensely satisfying.

8.2.   Strategy n.2: The Four-Box Method: Keep, Donate, Trash, Consider

The Four-Box Method is a tried-and-true decluttering method admired for its ease of use and effectiveness. This strategy enables a more simplified and targeted decluttering experience by breaking down your decision-making process into four separate actions. The Four-Box Method can be used in the context of Swedish Death Cleaning in the following ways:

Begin by setting up four large boxes or containers, each labeled as follows: "Keep," "Donate," "Trash," and "Consider."

★ **Keep Box**: These things are obviously valuable to you, either because you use them frequently, they have unique sentimental worth to you, or they are necessary for day-to-day survival. Put things you want to keep in this box as you go through your possessions.

★ **Donate Box**: This is where things that are still in good condition but are no longer useful in your life belong. Consider misfitting clothing, duplicate kitchenware, or novels you've read but don't intend to reread. Donating allows these goods to live again with someone who might find a purpose for them.

★ **Trash Box**: Put anything damaged, out-of-date, or beyond repair in this box. Recall that reducing waste is the main objective. Think about whether it can be fixed, upcycled, or at least parts of it recycled before tossing it out.

★ **Consider Box**: Items that you're unsure of go in this box. You may not have used them recently, but you may need them in the future. Or maybe they have sentimental worth, which makes the decision to let go a little more complicated. You can temporarily store these items in the "Consider" box and return to them after some thought.

Once you've sorted your items into these four boxes, take the following steps:

Immediate Action: Items from the "Keep" box should be stored where they belong. Find nearby organizations, shelters, or community centers that could use your stuff for the "Donate" box. When disposing of the "Trash" box, be responsible and prioritize recycling.

Reflection Period: The "Consider" box is unique because it requires a waiting period. Seal up this box and set a reminder for a month from now. The choice may become more obvious if the emotional or perceived benefit of these products has diminished. It may be worthwhile to store some objects for a little while longer if, after this time, you still have questions about them. If you've decided you can live without them, it's time to transfer them to the "Donate" or "Trash" box.

The Four-Box Method ensures that every item is addressed with intention by compartmentalizing the decluttering process. It can be a powerful tool in your quest for a decluttered, more conscious living area when combined with the concepts of Swedish Death Cleaning.

8.2.1. How to utilize the method effectively

Döstädning's philosophy strongly emphasizes introspection and making conscious decisions about what matters most. It involves figuring out what has value rather than throwing stuff away. The Four-Box Method shines brilliantly in this introspective setting. Its built-in reflection phase, best exemplified by the "Consider" box, perfectly aligns with Swedish Death Cleaning principles.

Start by making sure you have sturdy boxes or containers when getting ready to employ this technique. Putting these boxes in the center of the area you're clearing out of the clutter is essential. By strategically placing items, you may categorize them effectively as you go through them without the process feeling disconnected. A sense of development is encouraged by using an organized approach, such as starting in the wardrobe while cleaning the bedroom, then on to the bedside tables, and finally under the bed. Such a systematic approach guarantees that no detail is overlooked and stops the feeling of encroaching chaos.

Setting the proper atmosphere for decluttering is more crucial than it may first appear. You can increase your focus by setting aside certain hours for the activity and avoiding outside distractions. This can entail turning off your phone's notifications, telling your family members what you're planning, or creating a serene atmosphere with relaxing background music and plenty of natural light. Such a setting makes decluttering more convenient; it transforms it into a calming, almost meditative activity.

Especially in the context of Döstädning, the emotional landscape of decluttering might be difficult. Things may evoke intense emotions, particularly those that are connected to fond memories. While respecting these feelings is crucial, one must be watchful not to let them immobilize them. Consider placing anything in the "Consider" box if it causes prolonged thought. By doing this, you maintain momentum and avoid becoming stagnant.

Reviewing the items in the boxes from time to time, particularly those marked "Keep" and "Consider," can provide new insights. After some thought, a thing that formerly seemed essential could seem less important. When in question about specific goods, getting advice from trusted friends or relatives might be helpful. Sometimes, their objective perspective can restore clarity when emotions have clouded judgment.

It's also important to consider the temptation of returning to the "Consider" box too soon. But in this case, patience is a virtue. Giving yourself the designated reflection time can make the difference between making a choice you'll later regret and one you're confident about.

The Four-Box Method is, at its core, a journey rather than a destination. Understanding the worth and significance of possessions is more important than quickly achieving a decluttered environment. The technique is made even more effective when combined with the Döstädning's reflective nature. It's not only about making room organized; it's about creating a home that truly reflects who you are and the future you expect to achieve.

8.3. Strategy n.3: The One-Year Rule

The One-Year Rule is well-known in the world of decluttering. It provides a simple framework: if something hasn't been used or worn in a year, it could be time to let it go. Despite the rule's apparent attractiveness, it's important to comprehend its intricacies. This temporal criterion cannot be used to evaluate every possession. Some things call for a more thorough examination, weighing utility with emotion or prospective future value. We'll look at applying this principle wisely, ensuring that our decluttering choices fit our individual lifestyles, values, and situations.

8.3.1. If you haven't used/worn it in a year, consider letting it go.

Adopting a simple rule like "If you haven't used/worn it in a year, consider letting it go" can be pretty helpful in our search for a decluttered existence. Even though it is a straightforward concept, it forces us to consider our habits of consumption and retention, tests our attachment to material possessions, and encourages us to distinguish between need and want.

Let's begin with our wardrobes, frequently the focal point of accumulated items. Many items sit unused and forgotten, from that impulsively purchased jumper to those shoes that were a great deal but never quite fit correctly. By adhering to this criterion, it is simpler to determine which goods fit our present style and way of life. hose clothes that remain unworn often represent past phases, aspirations, or even regrets. Letting them go can be both a physical and emotional liberation, making room for items that truly complement our present identity.

This idea is valid not just for clothing but also for other household things. If kitchen appliances, electronics, or even books go unused for a year, it's important to consider their function. Are they useful, or are they just taking up valuable space? Adopting this guideline doesn't imply having a rigid mindset, though. Every object, after all, has a unique history. For instance, an item of clothing from a special occasion might be imbued with memories. In these circumstances, the rule operates more as a guideline, a prod towards reflection, than as a binding decree.

The one-year rule's beauty is its natural call to mindfulness. It helps us be present in our decisions, understand our changing tastes, and acknowledge worldly possessions' transience. We engage on a journey of self-awareness by constantly examining and reevaluating our possessions, ensuring that our surroundings resonate with who we genuinely are, eliminating the excess, and embracing the essentials.

8.3.2.   Exceptions to the rule and how to address them.

While the one-year rule is a useful guideline for many aspects of our lives, it is important to recognize that it may not apply to every case. Certain items have greater significance or have purposes that do not neatly correspond with a yearly calendar. Recognizing and addressing these exceptions can make the decluttering process more nuanced and adapted to individual requirements.

1.   **Seasonal Items:**

The one-year limit may not be appropriate for seasonal items.

Winter jackets, holiday decorations, and camping equipment are examples of items used infrequently but have indisputable utility.

Recommendation: Instead of annually, evaluate these possessions for wear and tear, relevancy, or changing personal preferences every few years.

2. **Sentimental Items:**

Items like jewelry passed down through generations or letters from loved ones may not see "regular use" yet have tremendous emotional significance.

Approach: Handle such items carefully, rethinking their storage or display rather than disposing of them after a year.

3. **Collectibles and Hobby-Related Items:**

Stamps, rare books, and musical instruments are examples of collections that are not frequently accessed but have emotional and financial significance.

Suggestion: Periodic evaluations based on changing interests or market values may be more appropriate than a yearly assessment.

4. **Items Kept for Potential Future Needs:**

Some items, like baby clothes for a future child or professional apparel for potential job interviews, are kept because they will be used in the future.

Approach: Determine the realistic probability of these events occurring; nevertheless, a one-year rule may not be feasible.

8.4. Strategy n.4: Tackling Sentimental Items

Sentimental items are typically the most difficult to deal with throughout decluttering. The strong feelings and memories associated with these things, whether old love letters or children's artwork have a special place in our hearts. Swedish Death Cleaning, although advocating for a less materialistic way of life, also values these emotional relationships. This chapter will examine the delicate balance of cherishing memories while establishing a serene, decluttered living environment.

Every person has items with significant emotional significance, even if they do not serve a functional role on a daily basis. Döstädning illuminates the memory or feeling associated with an item rather than the physical object itself. This comprehension provides a new viewpoint on how to treat such items.

Memory archives are an excellent approach to keeping memories without creating physical clutter. Digitizing these memories can help to bridge the gap between the past and the present. Photographing sentimental items or creating a digital scrapbook of treasured letters and documents might capture their spirit without requiring each item to be kept.

A designated memory box can be a powerful tool for extracting what is truly important. The goal is to select a separate container or box for items with significant sentimental value. Working with a guideline is beneficial: if the box begins to overflow and there is a desire to add another piece, it indicates that something else may need to find a new place. This practice guarantees that you always reflect on the items that truly resonate with you.

The decision to keep items frequently originates from the thought that they may be meaningful to our loved ones. Open discussions can reveal whether these items genuinely mean much to family or friends, influencing decisions concerning their retention. The idea behind decluttering sentimental items is to keep the feeling or memory without necessarily preserving the physical item. Techniques such as telling someone the narrative behind an object, photographing it, or simply remembering about it can be just as fulfilling.

Decluttering treasured items is a profoundly personal experience. It necessitates a delicate balance of respect for the past while making way for the present and future. The ultimate goal is not to abandon the past but to live in the present more fully, free of overpowering material attachments.

8.4.1. Why these are the hardest to declutter.

Sentimental items are special in our hearts because they provide physical reminders of fond memories, prior accomplishments, or lost loved ones. The profound emotional connections we create with these artifacts make them especially difficult to let go of. The fear of losing the memory associated with an object, the perceived obligation to inherited or gifted items, and the emotional toll of recalling specific memories all complicate decluttering such belongings. As we go further, we'll look at how to approach these items with empathy and intention to honor the memories while decluttering.

8.4.2. Strategies to keep memories without holding onto every item.

Our treasured possessions frequently bear strong emotional imprints, and it's normal to feel attached to them. However, as the core of Döstädning reminds us, it is the memory and sentiment, not the tangible object, that truly matters. Here are some ideas for preserving and honoring those priceless memories without clinging to every item:

Documentation: Photos are one of the most effective ways to remember the worth of valuable items. You can capture the essence of cherished items or heartfelt letters by photographing or scanning them. Digital memories take up little space and are instantly accessible, allowing you to relive them whenever you want.

The process of transforming items into something new may sometimes be cathartic. Take a look at the following:

Repurposing: Old clothes or blankets, for example, can be transformed into useful items such as quilts. These redesigned items frequently convey the same, if not stronger, sentiment. Similarly, heritage jewelry can be rebuilt or melted down to create a new item that retains the emotional worth of the original.

Curated Collections: We occasionally wind ourselves amassing enormous collections of items that are meaningful to us. On the other hand, choosing a few representative pieces to highlight can be more important. This not only declutters your environment but also ensures that your treasured memories are visible and not buried away.

Inherited Items: Objects passed down over generations, such as furniture or decor, carry a legacy. While they are significant, they must be considered concerning your current life and style. An object that may not appeal to you may find greater appreciation and usage elsewhere.

Emotional Clarity: Understand that giving up an object does not imply giving up the related memory. The fundamental purpose is to cherish memories and experiences free of physical clutter. Embracing this mindset will open the road for you to create a space that truly reflects your feelings and values.

8.4.3. Creating memory boxes or digital archives.

How to preserve the memories connected to sentimental goods is a problem we frequently run across in our quest for a decluttered and harmonious living space. Although we understand the value of removing physical clutter, these items' mental burden is evident. The answer is digital archives and memory boxes. For those priceless moments, stories, and feelings, both options provide a compact, organized, and accessible means to save them.

Select cherished items are kept in a memory box, a dedicated container frequently exquisitely made or creatively painted. Toys from childhood, dried flowers from memorable occasions, letters, postcards, and any other small souvenir that stirs up strong memories can all fall under this category. The objective is to preserve a carefully picked collection that truly reflects the essence of your journey rather than to keep everything. Each time you open this box, you enter a time capsule that offers a direct and personal connection to your past.

On the other hand, as technology has developed, digital archives have grown in popularity. Digital copies of sentimental objects are stored in these virtual, sometimes cloud-based locations. Here, old clothing can be photographed before being donated, handwritten notes can be scanned, and old recordings and movies can even be converted to digital form. A digital archive's accessibility and less physical footprint make it so beautiful. These memories can also be kept secure from any loss or harm using contemporary encryption and backup systems.

However, the fundamental idea is the same whether you decide on a memory box, a digital archive, or a combination of both: It's about cherishing memories, not clutter. These techniques allow us to recall, consider, and relive without filling our living environments. They link our history and the present, ensuring that our surroundings continue to represent who we are right now. As you begin your Swedish Death Cleaning adventure, these tools can be your allies, ensuring that no memory is left behind as you purge.

Note to the reader: see also chapter 8.7.3 for more information

8.5. Strategy n.5: Establishing Zones in Your Space

In interior organization, zoning turns areas into more useful and effective places suited to particular jobs or activities. By setting up distinct zones, you are improving your house's flow and ensuring that everything has a place and a function.

Consider the kitchen, for example. You may streamline the cooking and cleaning processes by creating prep zones near the cutting boards and knives, cooking zones near the stove with necessary utensils, and cleaning zones near the sink with detergents and scrubbers. Doing it this way means you won't have to walk around looking for things all the time. Instead, everything you require to complete a particular work is within reach. Zoning has advantages that go beyond practicality, such as psychological ones. Spaces grow cozier and less intimidating. Knowing that every room in your house serves a specific function can be mentally calming and help you cope with the tension from cluttered, unclear places.

Zoning begins with observation of your regular activities. Observe the trends: where do you frequently read? Maybe that should be your reading area, with a comfortable chair, good lighting, and a nearby book rack. The flexibility of zoning is another crucial component. Our requirements and routines change as life does. For a season, the reading area may become a workout corner. Your home should meet your current needs and your old routines, so you should be willing to adjust.

Your living space ultimately evolves into a setting where efficiency and relaxation are prioritized by creating and maintaining zones. It turns into a spotless, thoughtful, and clutter-free space that embodies Swedish Death Cleaning's guiding principles.

8.5.1. The idea of having specific zones for specific activities/items.

The concept of zoning in an interior organization is akin to compartmentalizing aspects of our life.. Similar to how our minds set aside distinct times for work, play, and personal time, our living environments can also be set up to correspond with our daily activities.

Zoning is fundamentally about logical organization. Imagine entering a room and automatically understanding where everything is and where it should be. This is what zoning aims to accomplish. When we speak of a "reading zone" or a "crafting zone," we don't simply mean a location where these activities occur; we also mean a space created to encourage and promote that activity. For instance, having a chair and a lamp in a reading area is insufficient. The atmosphere, a nearby bookcase, a cozy throw blanket for cooler days, or a little table to set a cup of tea on are all important factors. Each element in that space aims to improve the reading experience.

Similarly, a crafting zone might have sufficient supply storage, appropriate lighting, and a sizable table impervious to spills and cuts. Intentionality is ultimately what zoning is about. It involves taking a moment to reflect on what you truly want from each space in your house. Zoning requires you to plan your spaces carefully rather than letting them develop randomly based on haphazard purchases or transient demands. Since everything has a place, this makes daily tasks more enjoyable and makes maintenance and tidying easier.

8.5.2. How this method can help in maintaining a decluttered space.

After all, it's not just about providing a chair and a lamp in a reading zone. It's about the atmosphere, the neighboring bookcase, the cozy throw blanket for cooler days, or the tiny table on which to set a cup of tea. To improve the reading experience, every component in that zone was carefully selected. Similarly, a crafting zone may be furnished with sufficient supply storage, appropriate lighting, and a sizable table that is resistant to spills and cuts.

Intentionality is ultimately what zoning is about. It's about taking a moment to think about what you want from each space in your house. Zoning requires you to plan your spaces carefully rather than letting them develop randomly based on random purchases or transient demands. Since everything has a place, this makes daily activities more fun and makes maintenance and decluttering easier.

8.6.   Strategy n.6: Recycling, Upcycling, and Disposal

Making sure to take a careful approach to decluttering entails managing the items you decide to part with appropriately in addition to choosing what to keep. How you dispose of unwanted items is equally important in light of the growing global emphasis on sustainability and waste reduction.

8.6.1: Responsible Disposal of Items

It's important to undertake the decluttering process with consideration for the environment. Always ask yourself if you can reuse, donate, or recycle something before throwing it in the garbage. When items can still be processed and used or have a useful lifespan, they frequently end up in landfills. The first step in ethical disposal is determining whether products are recyclable and local recycling regulations.

8.6.2: Ideas for Upcycling Items into Something New and Useful

Upcycling is the creative process of transforming waste materials or unwanted items into new, higher-quality products with new uses. Before you throw something out, consider its potential uses instead:

❖ You may make tote bags or quilts out of old T-shirts.

❖ You may create rustic furniture from wooden pallets.

❖ Glass jars are used as storage containers and beautiful vases.

Items intended for the trash can be repurposed with a little imagination, conserving resources and reducing waste.

8.6.3: Resources and Places to Donate Unwanted Items

Donating is a beautiful way to assist those in need while giving your items a second life. Before throwing something out, consider whether it might be useful to someone else. There is always a desire for clothing, toys, books, and household items.

● Many local organizations and shelters accept nicely used items.

● Schools and community centers could value books or art supplies.

● Magazines or puzzles could be useful in hospitals or nursing homes.

Keep in mind that Swedish Death Cleaning aims not just to declutter but to do it in a way that respects the value of each object, whether by repurposing, recycling, or gifting it to someone else. This chapter essentially emphasizes that just because an object no longer fits into your life doesn't mean that its journey must come to an end.

8.7. Strategy n.7: Emotional Inventory Check: Releasing Sentimental Items

Letting go of personal items, especially ones that hold memories, can be a difficult part of decluttering. These items, even if they no longer serve a useful purpose, frequently serve as anchors to moments, people, or feelings from our past.

8.7.1: Strategies to Detach While Honoring Memories

While it is natural to identify objects with memories, it is critical to remember that the memories reside within us, not in the objects. Consider the following strategies:

Narrative Approach: Discuss or write about an object before letting it go. Tell about the memory linked with it. This captures the sentiment and may make it simpler to release the object.

Capture Digitally: Consider photographing items that are difficult to store but have emotional worth. Digital albums can function as a compact and easily accessible memory vault.

Token System: Instead of keeping all items from an event or person, select one representative token and let go of the rest.

8.7.2: Overcoming Emotional Barriers

We may hold onto items out of guilt, loss, or the hope of returning to a more idealized version of ourselves, among other motives. Making logical decisions can help with these feelings by understanding them:

Gift Guilt: Just because something was a gift doesn't mean you have to keep using it forever. Recognize the love and the sentiment, but let go if it doesn't benefit you.

Loss Association: It might be difficult to leave with things that once belonged to a lost loved one. But ask yourself if holding on to everything keeps you from moving forward.

8.7.3: Creating Memory Boxes

Making a "Memory Box" is a practical way to keep sentimental items safe without producing an overabundance of clutter. The most cherished mementos can be kept in this compact container:

Curation: Revisit the box regularly. If it begins to overflow, it's a reminder to select and save the most priceless memories.

Sharing Stories: Share stories with younger generations using the items in the memory box. These items now serve a new purpose in addition to helping to preserve family history.

In the end, cherishing the memory should take precedence over necessarily loving the thing that brought it on. Swedish Death Cleaning can help you let go while maintaining sentiments close to your heart through conscious tactics and emotional introspection.

8.8. Strategy n.8: Enlisting Help: When and How to Involve Loved Ones

Starting the Swedish Death Cleaning path is not just a personal endeavor; it frequently touches on the lives of our loved ones. Involving family and friends may be both a blessing and a difficulty, whether selecting what to do with shared possessions, traversing emotional terrains, or just looking for support.

8.8.1: Navigating Emotions and Disagreements

It's natural for disagreements to arise while decluttering communal places or communal items. Remember that everyone defines worth in their own unique way; therefore, what one person may deem unimportant to them may hold great emotional significance to another. Open communication is essential. The justifications for maintaining or letting go of particular items should be discussed. The bigger goal of creating a peaceful, decluttered space that everyone may enjoy should be highlighted. When feelings have subsided, taking breaks or revisiting specific decisions might occasionally be beneficial.

8.8.2: Seeking Input on Sentimental Items

Shared memories are often associated with particular items. It's kind to ask individuals who could also connect emotionally to the items before discarding them. A family heirloom, for instance, might not hold particular significance to you personally, but it might to another family member. You can ensure that items with true sentimental worth go to the correct home by asking for feedback and respecting and acknowledging the shared emotional landscape.

8.8.3: Collaborative Sessions

Collaborative decluttering sessions can be good. Shared viewpoints can clarify what to preserve and what to release in addition to dividing the task, making it less intimidating. Rotate between the duties throughout these sessions so that one person is sorting, one is making choices, and one is handling disposal. This rotation can ensure that everyone's opinions are considered and that work is never repetitive.

8.8.4: Celebrating Milestones Together

Every significant achievement in the decluttering process deserves praise. Celebrate achievements with your loved ones, whether finishing a challenging space's decluttering or just staying the course for a set period. These events encourage everyone to be engaged and remind them of the advantages of their combined efforts. Everyone can benefit when loved ones participate in the Swedish Death Cleaning procedure. It makes relationships stronger, promotes the sharing of memories, and cultivates an atmosphere of comprehension and cooperation. There will be difficulties, but working together frequently yields more significant and long-lasting results.

8.9.   Strategy n. 9: Preventing Future Clutter

Swedish Death Cleaning is about keeping that clarity and simplicity throughout time, not just about decluttering once. The true challenge is ensuring that clutter doesn't return after a space has been decluttered. Let's look at some methods for keeping your space continuously harmonious and preventing the collection of unneeded items.

8.9.1: Habits to Develop to Prevent Accumulation

The cornerstone of prevention is awareness. Develop a routine of introspection before making purchases. Consider whether the item enhances your life rather than just satisfying a momentary craving. Put quality over number by choosing items with numerous uses and a longer lifespan to reduce the need for replacements or extra items.

The "one in, one out" rule is another crucial behavior. Take out everything similar whenever you introduce a new item into your space. This practice encourages you to critically evaluate the value of new acquisitions while maintaining the equilibrium of your things.

8.9.2: Setting up Monthly or Quarterly Decluttering Routines

The secret to avoiding clutter is consistency. You may notice any clutter buildup early on by scheduling a set time—whether monthly or quarterly—to assess your stuff. These sessions don't have to last very long; sometimes, a simple inspection of your space might reveal problem areas.

These routines for periodic decluttering turn into a type of self-care. They provide moments of introspection, enabling you to reconnect with your values and ensuring that your environment continues to mirror your intentions.

8.9.3: Conscious Consumerism

It's simple to be persuaded into purchasing items we don't need in today's consumerist society. Making judgments about what to buy consistent with your personal and environmental values is part of practicing conscious consumption. It entails being conscious of how your consumption affects the larger environment as well as just your personal space.

Investigate a product's durability and versatility before purchasing. Encourage ethical and sustainable brands. By exercising deliberate decision-making, you lessen the influx of superfluous items and favorably impact more general world challenges.

8.9.4: Designated Spaces for Everything

Having a space for everything is a straightforward but efficient method. Everything having a place to go lessens the possibility of random items accumulating. Additionally, it makes it simpler to recognize when something doesn't belong or when an area is being overcrowded. A little daily routine that can go a long way towards keeping order is regularly returning items to their proper space.

The Swedish Death Cleaning journey aims to create a clutter-free environment rather than just to declutter. You can ensure that your space continues to reflect the serenity and purposefulness inherent in the Swedish Death Cleaning philosophy by incorporating these practices into your daily life.

We will elaborate further on this concept in the next chapter

Chapter 9. Maintaining Your Decluttered Sanctuary

As we already mentioned, after you've decluttered your space and experienced the liberating feeling it brings, the next crucial step is ensuring the maintenance of this newfound sanctuary. A decluttered space is only as good as its continued upkeep.

9.1. Scheduling regular reassessments

Any transformation that is intended to be long-lasting must begin with consistency as its foundation. Swedish Death Cleaning is not a one-time event but a marathon that requires regular assessments to ensure that its core remains intact. Your space may have become more serene due to the decluttering process; nevertheless, to keep it that way, you will need to conduct routine assessments.

Consider the following: To ensure your car runs well, you have it serviced. Minor problems might turn into serious ones if they are ignored for a long time. Similar maintenance is required for your home environment to stop the creeping onset of chaos.

Regular evaluations need not include a laborious cleaning or decluttering session. Instead, consider them as chances to:

Realign with your goals: Your lifestyle or ambitions may change over time. Regular check-ins let you make the necessary adjustments to your space.

Address small clutter accumulations: There will always be some clutter from day-to-day existence. During your future reassessments, address it rather than letting it grow.

Revise storage solutions: It's possible that a particular storage strategy isn't helping you as much as you anticipated. Regular reviews give you a chance to adjust and improve.

Reflect on your relationship with items: You can discover over time that something you once considered important doesn't hold up either. Regular reassessments grant the freedom to let go.

You can choose the frequency of these reassessments based on your preferences. While some people might think monthly checkups are sufficient, others would like a seasonal or biannual approach. The most important thing is to schedule and incorporate them into your daily routine.

9.2.   Mindful purchasing: questions to ask before acquiring new items

Not just what we remove but also what we add to our environment plays a crucial role in keeping our space decluttered. Swedish Death Cleaning emphasizes both the purging of unneeded items and the development of a mindful consuming style.

The modern world constantly barrages us with marketing, offering things as fixes for issues we weren't even aware we had. This relentless consumerism might swiftly diminish the advantages of complete decluttering. However, one can achieve a harmonious balance between the requirements and the excess by developing an attitude of conscious consumption.

It's helpful to pause and ask yourself some insightful questions before adding a new item to your space:

1. **Is it a Need or a Want?**

It is possible to avoid impulsive purchases by distinguishing between genuine needs and mere wants. Things in the "want" category aren't always negative but need more thought.

2. **How Often Will I Use It?**

Even a genuine need can gather dust if you don't use it frequently. If it justifies its space, think about how frequently it is used.

3. **Where Will It Live?**

Consider a precise location for the item in your home before purchasing. Consider your options if you can't visualize where it will fit perfectly.

4. **Does It Replace Something?**

Ensure you're willing to let go of the older version if the new item performs the same role as something you already own. Maintaining a decluttered space can be greatly aided by the "one in, one out" guideline.

5. **How Long Will It Last?**

Choose quality above quantity. Even though they may cost more upfront, durable goods can help you save money and reduce clutter.

6. **What's the Return Policy?**

Your security net can be a good return policy. It grants the freedom to reconsider the purchase after the first allure has faded.

7. **Am I Being Influenced?**

Recognize the influence of outside factors, such as peer pressure, advertising, or passing trends. Make sure your purchasing choices are based on genuine needs or desires.

You strengthen the sanctity of your decluttered space by incorporating these inquiries into your purchase practice. By preventing the invasion of pointless items, mindful shopping helps to keep your home a reflection of your intentionality and purpose.

9.3.   Celebrating milestones and honoring your space

It's crucial to pause and reflect on the wins as the decluttering process progresses. Swedish Death Cleaning is a way of life that emphasizes celebrating the transformational journey and true adoration of the space you've created. It's not just about removal and mindfulness.

The Joy of Achieved Milestones

You get closer to a living environment that breathes tranquility, meaning, and joy with every step you take in this decluttering project, no matter how big or tiny. Maybe you've finally given away your old magazine collection, converted a chaotic space into a tranquil reading corner, or resisted the impulse to purchase an enticing but useless item. These are accomplishments deserving of praise.

Each achievement represents a mental and emotional transformation in addition to just the physical act of decluttering. All admirable accomplishments are the ability to let go bravely, use discernment, and resist impulsively.

Honoring Your Sanctuary

A home is more than just the items you keep inside; it's a refuge where you may create memories, laugh and cry, and escape the outside world. You've created a space that genuinely reflects your values and objectives as you've decluttered and made deliberate decisions about what to keep and what to add.

To honor this space:

Regularly Refresh: Be careful to maintain periodically your living area in addition to the initial decluttering task. A monthly check can be helpful to find any places that might be returning to clutter.

Add Personal Touches: Introduce décor or items that have particular meaning to the person, such as a photograph, memento, or work of art. These items should remind you of cherished memories or dreams, which should improve your mood.

Cultivate Moments of Reflection: Sit in your favorite chair occasionally. Enjoy the peace and allow your thankfulness for your decluttered space to wash over you. These reflective moments might serve as strong reinforcements for the adventure you've started.

Share Your Space: Invite friends or family over, not to show off, but to share the peace and joy your home offers. The shared experiences can further embed positive associations with your living space.

Not to show off, but to share the calm and happiness your home brings, invite friends or family. The shared experiences may further cement positive associations with your living space.

Chapter 10. Beyond Physical Clutter: Navigating the Digital Realm

The virtual space we occupy in today's technologically advanced society often serves as a mirror of the real world. Our digital lives can turn into a maze of useless files, forgotten apps, and never-ending notifications, just as our houses can become cluttered with pointless items. Despite taking up no real physical space, these invisible responsibilities can still be very heavy on our minds. Swedish Death Cleaning's guiding principles, normally applied to our material possessions, are equally applicable in this digital age. In this chapter, we set out to comprehend the subtleties of digital clutter and how Döstädning's tranquility and intentionality might lead us to a more peaceful online existence.

10.1. Recognizing and addressing digital clutter

Our laptops, smartphones, and other digital accounts have become essential extensions of our identities. They save our emails, papers, and other things. But much like with other possessions, our plethora of digital content can quickly turn into a disorganized mess. Modern life presents a challenge of digital clutter, but it's more than just having too many files; it's about how these digital belongings can affect our mental health, productivity, and entire digital experience.

Think about how often you've become frustrated trying to sort through a packed email inbox or struggling to identify a specific photo among thousands. A disorganized digital space might generate similar feelings of tension as a messy physical space. Digital clutter is often subtle but equally taxing. There are several signs that it could be time for digital decluttering, including sluggish device performance, persistent difficulty finding key files, a desktop cluttered with icons, or feeling overwhelmed while opening your email.

Yet, why do we let our digital spaces get to this point? The apparent limitlessness of digital storage is one of the causes. It's simple to miss when clutter isn't there. As with real items, we don't see the pile expanding. However, the consequences are present, quietly impairing our digital experience.

It becomes clear that decluttering our digital lives isn't only about freeing up storage space when we adopt the Swedish Death Cleaning attitude. It's about creating a digital environment that fits our values, needs, and priorities. It's about making a space where we can interact, work, and play without feeling constrained. We're taking the first, most important step towards implementing Döstädning principles in our online life by recognizing the existence and effects of digital clutter. We'll go deeper into tactics for streamlining and preserving our digital spaces as we go along so that they support our productivity and well-being.

10.2. Applying Swedish Death Cleaning principles to digital spaces

The core of Döstädning is conscious decluttering, curating our surroundings, and leaving behind a legacy free of pointless responsibilities. Even though the idea was developed with the physical world in mind, its fundamentals are remarkably applicable and adaptable to our digital environments.

Intentionality and Purpose: Döstädning's primary premise is to only surround ourselves with items that have a function or make us happy. This entails critically analyzing our digital assets, such as our files, apps, and other assets, critically. There's no reason to keep old files or unwanted applications around, just as we wouldn't maintain a drawer full of useless items. Check your devices' and cloud services' storage frequently. Keep only what is essential and meaningful, and let the rest go.

Legacy Thinking: Swedish Death Cleaning makes us think about the legacy we're leaving behind for future generations. This includes our tangible possessions and digital footprint in the modern world. Think about all the pictures, papers, and online accounts. Do you know how to access essential files or accounts if needed? Would they comprehend the significance of them? By organizing and decluttering our digital possessions, we not only improve our own lives but also that of those we leave behind.

Mindful Consumption: We should apply this knowledge to our digital behavior like Döstädning encourages thoughtful consumption in the real world. Consider your options carefully before downloading a new app, subscribing to a newsletter, or storing another file. Do you genuinely need it? Will it improve your life or just add to your digital clutter?

Simple Organization: Swedish Death Cleaning is fundamentally about organizing items. Similarly, a well-organized digital environment can increase our productivity and calmness. Utilise file naming conventions, make clear folder hierarchies, and regularly backup vital data. Every digital file should have a logical position in your digital space, just as every physical item in your home should have a specified location.

Revisiting and Reflecting: Döstädning is a continual process rather than a singular event. Similar to physical decluttering, digital decluttering requires ongoing effort. To ensure your digital spaces align with your needs and values, set aside time every so often to revisit and review them.

In the following sections, we'll look at practical tools and approaches for dealing with digital clutter. However, just as with any decluttering process, the mindset with which you approach the task is critical. The idea isn't just about freeing up storage space, remember. It is about establishing a digital environment fostering clarity, purpose, and meaningful connections.

10.3. Tools and methods for streamlined online living

The quantity of online tools, platforms, and information available in the digital age might be daunting. However, just as we strive to make our physical places lean and purposeful with Döstädning, we can apply the same idea to our digital domain. This section will introduce you to various tools and approaches for streamlining your online life and ensuring that your digital space complements your quest for a simpler and more meaningful life.

Digital Decluttering Platforms: Software and apps are available to assist in identifying duplicate files, cleaning out unwanted applications, and optimizing storage. CleanMyMac™ for Mac users and CCleaner™ for Windows users are two examples. Such programs can give you an overview of what's taking up space and help you decide what to keep and toss.

Password Managers: We amass a variety of online accounts over time. It might be difficult to remember each password, let alone ensure that each is unique and secure. Password managers, such as LastPass™ or

1Password™, not only securely store passwords but also generate and fill them for you, easing your online navigation.

Digital Note Organizers: Platforms such as Evernote™ and Microsoft OneNote™ can be extremely helpful in decluttering your digital note-taking. To keep your notes, lists, and ideas organized and easily accessible, they provide a centralized space.

Photo Organization Tools: Digital images often add significantly to our digital clutter. Platforms such as Google Photos™ and Apple's Photos™ app provide capabilities for organizing, backing up, and even recognizing faces or objects, making photo administration a pleasure. Review and eliminate redundant or unnecessary photos regularly to keep your digital memories concise and meaningful.

Email Unsubscribers: Email clutter can be exhausting, as inboxes get overburdened with newsletters, advertising, and other unsolicited material. Unroll.Me™, for example, may help you unsubscribe from unwanted email lists in bulk, ensuring that only meaningful correspondence reaches you.

Digital Minimalist Browsers: Browsers like Brave and Firefox Focus prioritize privacy, speed, and a clutter-free surfing experience by removing extraneous elements and trackers.

Decluttering Your Social Media: Review the profiles you follow on sites like Instagram, Twitter, and Facebook regularly. Rather than mindless scrolling, make your feed a source of inspiration, education, or genuine connection.

While these tools and strategies can significantly assist you in your digital decluttering journey, your intentions are at the heart of the process. Set aside time regularly to analyze and trim your digital areas. By cultivating a healthy balance between your life's tangible and intangible components, you mirror the ideas of Döstädning by maintaining a curated and organized digital environment.

10.4: Step-by-step Digital Declutter Method

Decluttering our online environments has become as important as tidying our physical surroundings in an age when our lives are increasingly connected with the digital world. While technologies and platforms can help, a systematic approach ensures a thorough and long-lasting impact. Here's a step-by-step guide to decluttering your digital life:

1. Set Clear Objectives:

Determine why you want to declutter before you begin. Is it to boost productivity? Maybe to eliminate distractions or free up storage space? Having specific goals will help you make selections as you filter through digital content.

2. Start with a Backup:

Before you begin a digital decluttering project, ensure you've backed up all your important data. External hard drives and cloud storage solutions such as Google Drive™ or Dropbox™ can be useful.

3. Tackle One Device at a Time:

Focus on one device before going on to the next, whether it's your smartphone, laptop, tablet, or desktop. This enables a thorough evaluation without being overwhelmed.

4. Declutter Your Desktop:

Your computer's desktop is often a dumping ground for odd files, folders, and applications. Organise files into specified folders, eliminate unneeded items, and preserve just critical applications or often accessed files on the desktop.

5. Organize Your Documents:

Go through your 'Documents' folder and organize your files into distinct folders such as 'Finances,' 'Work Projects,' 'Personal,' and so on. Delete old files and use a consistent naming convention to make searching easier.

6. Clean Up Your Downloads:

Another hotspot for clutter is the 'Downloads' folder. Sort through and remove files that you no longer need regularly. Place crucial files in the appropriate folders.

7. Curate Your Photos and Videos:

Delete duplicates, hazy images, and pointless films. Put them in albums or folders according to the occasion, the day, or the topic. Think about utilizing software that finds and gets rid of duplicates.

8. Review Software and Apps:

Uninstall applications that you haven't used in a while. Only keep commonly used apps on your phone's home screen, and group apps into folders according to category.

9. Streamline Your Email:

Delete any newsletters or marketing communications that are no longer useful to you. Create folders or labels for your emails, and try to keep your inbox at or below zero by routinely responding to or archiving emails.

10. Declutter Social Media:

Take a look at the accounts you follow. Delete or mute accounts that don't support your goals or values. Remove outdated posts and pictures that don't represent who you are now.

11. Update Your Digital Security:

It's a good idea to increase your digital security while you declutter. Ensure your security software is current, update your passwords, and enable two-factor authentication.

12. Regular Maintenance:

Make it a point to periodically assess and declutter your digital places. Depending on your needs, this might happen monthly, quarterly, or every two years.

In addition to making your digital environments feel lighter and easier to manage, this step-by-step approach will make all your digital interactions more deliberate and purposeful, reflecting the Döstädning way of thinking.

Congratulations on your progress, and thank you for purchasing

this book.

Scan this QR CODE to download your printable bonus

OR COPY AND PASTE THE URL:

https://o2o.to/i/e5n4ti

Chapter 11: End of Life and Döstädning

Note to the reader: This chapter touches on the end-of-life aspect related to Döstädning in detail and is designed for those approaching this period of their life.

As we progressed through the earlier chapters, it became clear that Döstädning isn't just a decluttering technique; it's a mindset, a concept that goes well beyond our material possessions. We shall delve into how the Döstädning lifestyle's guiding principles can be incorporated into numerous parts of our lives in Chapter 12 as we examine the Döstädning lifestyle's greater scope. The essence of Döstädning can direct us in creating a life characterized by simplicity, intentionality, and purpose, from cultivating mindful relationships to making environmentally friendly decisions. This chapter offers tips to help you get the most out of the Döstädning way of life, whether trying to comprehend it better or how to apply its teachings in your daily life.

11.1. Understanding End of Life: A Brief Overview

Many of us would rather not talk about dying. It serves as a reminder of both the transience of life and the unavoidable passage of time, both present in our existence. Understanding the end of life, however, is not about depressing reflection or sorrow in the context of Swedish Death Cleaning; instead, it is about accepting and honoring the cyclical aspect of life.

Every culture and civilization has its rituals, traditions, and beliefs related to death. These rituals, which are often based on profound historical and spiritual settings, assist communities and individuals in accepting the impermanence of life while also remembering the contributions of the departed.

The idea of Döstädning has two meanings for Swedes. In the first place, it's a sensible strategy to prevent our passing from burdening our loved ones with pointless clutter or decisions. Second, it's a process of reflection, cherishing memories, and making peace with any unresolved issues. It is a form of emotional and spiritual preparation.

We might face Döstädning with a revitalized feeling of purpose by taking the time to comprehend the bigger picture implications of this subject. This is about creating an intentional space that honors our journey, experiences, and cherished moments; it's not just about cleaning up or decluttering. And by doing this, we ensure that our legacy will be one of attention, respect, and thankfulness, in whatever form it may take.

11.1.1. Cultural Views on Mortality

Culture is a critical factor in determining how we view life, death, and everything in between. Every civilization has left its distinctive stories, rituals, and ethos regarding the nature of mortality on the annals of history. These cultural perspectives shed light on how people have attempted to make sense of the unavoidable.

Many cultures view the end of life as merely a change from one state of existence to another. Think of the ancient Egyptians, who built magnificent pyramids, treasure-filled tombs, and complex mummification techniques in preparation for the afterlife. Their conviction was based on the notion that life continued after death, albeit in a different environment, and that death was but a door.

On the other hand, a fundamental premise of many Eastern philosophies is the cycle of birth, death, and reincarnation. Hinduism, for example, holds that the soul passes through multiple cycles of birth and rebirth, with each life resulting from the accumulated karma of the preceding ones. The goal then shifts to obtaining "moksha" or freedom from this cycle, which results in eternal peace. Judeo-Christian ideologies have had a significant impact on Western civilizations. As a result, people often view the end of life as a journey to Heaven or Hell, a place where one will spend eternity depending on one's actions while they are still on Earth. This eschatological perspective establishes a moral foundation for behavior, ethics, and values.

However, many of these viewpoints undergo cross-cultural exchanges as the globe becomes more globalized. A blending of beliefs and practices results from the blurring of the formerly distinct boundaries. Nevertheless, despite the diversity of opinions, there is a mostly shared understanding of how important it is to remember the deceased, honor their legacy, and bid them a respectful farewell.

The emphasis for the Swedes, and hence, the philosophy underlying Döstädning, is not just on the spiritual or metaphysical spheres. It is grounded in practicality, making sure one's affairs are in order, facilitating the transition for those left behind, and gracefully and mindfully facing mortality. While distinct in its implementation, this strategy reflects the universal human need to give death significance, respect, and permanence.

11.1.2. Embracing the Inevitability of Life's End

Existentialist thinkers often ponder end of life as the one certainty in an unpredictable life. The acceptance of mortality as an inevitable aspect of the human experience unites societies despite differences in rituals, beliefs, and stories around death. Instead of avoiding this inevitable, we should embrace it because it can significantly impact how we live.

Living constantly under the end of life's shadow can have its limitations. The anxiety can limit experiences, making us more risk-averse and less receptive to the myriad of opportunities life presents. However, a contradiction arises when we sincerely understand that end of life is inevitable. We can appreciate the transience of life by acknowledging it and cherishing each moment, connection, and experience with greater passion. This idea is prevalent in both literature and philosophy. For example, the ancient Greek stoics advocated daily reflections on mortality, not as a morbid activity but rather as a way to foster gratitude for the moment. Their guiding principle was memento mori, which means "remember that you will die," serving as a sobering reminder to live with virtue and intention.

Furthermore, accepting death can inspire us to take proactive steps to relieve our loved ones of their burdens following our passing. Döstädning finds its resonance in this area. By meticulously cleaning, decluttering, and organizing our possessions, we're not just tidying up; we're also leaving behind a considerate legacy, a sign that we cared enough to make the grieving process for those we leave behind a little bit easier. This is not to say that embracing end of life is simple. It's a trip with moments of existential angst and introspection. However, life's path might become more meaningful if one learns to accept it. When we face end of life head-on, we may refocus our efforts on building a life that will be remembered, ensuring that our finite time is spent on activities, connections, and experiences that matter.

11.2.   The Philosophy of Döstädning in End-of-Life Planning

Swedish Death Cleaning, or Döstädning, is more than just a way of decluttering; it's a concept that integrates with end-of-life considerations. This idea is about having compassion for oneself and people who will eventually handle our possessions when we go. It's a practice that acknowledges our obligation to lessen our loved ones' burdens and make their transition easier for them after we pass away.

Döstädning is a concept that extends beyond just material possessions in session. It goes in-depth on acceptance, comprehension, and introspection. Each object we own has memories, choices, and the echoes of experiences that have influenced our lives. Looking at each item we own, we see more than just a physical object. We are faced with the crucial quest of determining what matters as we start this decluttering journey.

Every item we choose to hold onto or let go of is a decision about how we want to be remembered. Do we want to be remembered for the selected collection of meaningful artifacts that tell a story about our passions, adventures, and the people we loved or for the hundreds of trinkets and souvenirs we've gathered over the years? The Döstädning method encourages us to talk to our loved ones and friends. It forces us to have uncomfortable but essential conversations about our last wishes, what we want done with our possessions, and how we picture our final days. With those we hold dear, this can be a highly intimate encounter that fosters understanding.

Döstädning is also, in a sense, about taking charge. So often, the end of life is connected to a loss of agency, a period when choices are made for us rather than by us. We reclaim some of our control by choosing how our story is conveyed and making sure that our narrative is clear, concise, and representative of who we truly are. Döstädning is a profound meditation on legacy at its heart. It makes us consider the imprints we leave behind, both tangible and intangible. This Swedish practice offers a holistic strategy for end-of-life planning that is firmly anchored in love, respect, and understanding by fusing the practicalities of decluttering with the profound contemplation of the end of life.

11.2.1. Preparing for a Tranquil Transition

Döstädning, or Swedish Death Cleaning, is not just about decluttering our physical spaces but also about getting ready for the final transition we will all experience. This chapter emphasizes how crucial it is to incorporate this distinctive Swedish practice into end-of-life preparation in order to ensure a peaceful and pain-free transition for both the person passing and their loved ones.

In the Swedish tradition, a profound respect for the transitory character of existence shapes how people face end of life. Döstädning is a vital component of end-of-life preparations because of this acceptance and a desire to lessen the difficulties of those left behind. This approach involves thankfulness, reflection, and awareness rather than negativity. A variety of feelings might surface when one begins to prepare for their eventual departure. These emotions can include fear, melancholy, and feelings of freedom and contentment. By proactively approaching end-of-life matters through the lens of Döstädning, we focus on the memories, experiences, and values we cherish most rather than on the inevitable end.

The following are key considerations when using Döstädning to prepare for a tranquil transition:

- ❖ **Recognizing What Truly Matters**: The clutter of pointless items and unfinished business can obfuscate what truly matters as we approach the end of our lives. Döstädning pushes us to prioritize the relationships, memories, and life lessons that are most cherished to us.

- ❖ **Communication:** We can avoid leaving our loved ones in the dark by communicating our wishes. This can include everything from how one wants to be remembered to how personal possessions should be distributed.

- ❖ **Embracing Legacy:** Even after we pass away, knowing that our life has an impact will be comforting. Döstädning helps define that legacy through treasured heirlooms, documented life stories, or values passed on to younger generations.

- ❖ **Reducing Stress for Loved Ones:** To reduce the emotional and practical load on those we leave behind is one of Döstädning's main goals. We avoid our families the burden of having to make these difficult choices during their grief by taking care of our possessions, affairs, and desires in advance.

Döstädning's approach to end-of-life preparation is a journey that balances our past, present, and future. It's a powerful technique that creates a peaceful transition and leaves a legacy of love, clarity, and gratitude.

11.2.2. The Deep Emotional Significance of Döstädning

Döstädning is more than just a method of decluttering; it is an emotional and spiritual journey woven into the very fabric of existence. Understanding its profound significance reveals a far deeper connection with life, memories, and eventual mortality, even though it may initially appear just a Swedish method of organizing and tidying up. The recognition of our mortality lies at the core of Döstädning. Accepting this somber yet profound realization enables us to change our perspective and highlight the precious aspects of our existence.

It encourages us to prioritize and cherish sincere moments by serving as a gentle reminder of life's transient nature.

More than just a physical effort, this journey of decluttering also serves as a vehicle for emotional release. When we part with items, we frequently do so symbolically with past regrets, guilts, or unresolved problems, which makes the act a means of healing and self-rediscovery. It becomes a concrete way to explore our inner landscapes and bring closure to our past experiences. The practice also offers opportunities for more in-depth connections and dialogue with loved ones. Restoring the value of an heirloom or recalling memories connected to particular items fosters shared reflections and strengthens family bonds.

Legacy is another important aspect of this process. Döstädning challenges us to reflect on our actions, the possessions we've amassed, the memories we've imprinted in the sands of time, and the material possessions we'll leave behind. It turns into a mirror that reflects our journey through life, the lessons we've learned, and the legacy we hope to leave behind. A cornerstone of this approach is being present. We develop a more profound sense of mindfulness as we interact with our possessions and the associated memories and decide what will happen to them. By bringing us back to the present moment and grounding us, this awareness highlights life's fleeting beauty.

Döstädning ultimately offers a way to resolution and peace. It ensures that everyone knows what we want in this life and the next, providing clarity and comfort to ourselves and those we leave behind. Döstädning's true beauty lies in its methodology and capacity to weave together the material and immaterial, producing a mellow symphony of life, memories, and the peace that comes from realizing our place in the vast web of existence.

11.3. Practical Steps in End of Life Planning with Döstädning

A mindful and compassionate approach is introduced to a subject frequently rife with sensitivity by the unique fusion of Swedish Death Cleaning and End of Life Planning. The task of making end-of-life arrangements becomes a therapeutic process that brings resolution and peace thanks to Döstädning's gentle view on mortality.

11.3.1. Starting Conversations with Loved Ones

A range of emotions are involved in the delicate process of confronting and talking about mortality. The Swedish Death Cleaning method, or Döstädning, rises to this challenge by starting heart-to-heart conversations grounded in respect, love, and understanding. This method's central tenet is the recognition that these conversations, despite being challenging, are essential for both practical and emotional reasons.

The end of life can be taboo in many cultures and shrouded in superstition, fear, or sadness. By serving as a conduit and a bridge over these societal divides, Döstädning turns the conversation into a celebration of life and its transient nature. In this process, open communication is crucial. It prepares loved ones for life's unforeseen circumstances and gives them assurances about your intentions, wishes, and the thinking behind particular choices. By removing any doubts, these discussions help avoid future misunderstandings or conflicts. Their legacy is one of clarity and love, paving the way for a more peaceful transition.

Finesse and empathy are needed to start the conversation. By choosing a setting that is calm, comfortable, and free of distractions, you can create the ideal atmosphere. A comfortable setting can help the subject seem more approachable. While it's important to be upfront about your goals, treat the subject with a certain amount of delicacy. Using sentences like "I've been thinking about the future and how I'd like things to be for everyone when I'm not around" can be a nice way to start a conversation. Asking for feedback and letting your loved ones express their emotions is also essential. While some may be receptive, others may be emotional or resistant. Recognize that every person approaches the idea of mortality differently. Additionally, since one conversation might not be sufficient, be ready to bring up the subject again and provide additional clarification or address any brand-new issues that may have come up.

While Döstädning strongly emphasizes open communication, maintaining boundaries is just as important. Giving someone you care about time is critical if they're not ready to have such a conversation. Pushing the issue might result in withdrawal or resentment. Instead, let them know you understand and be there for them whenever they're ready. When one begins the Döstädning journey, they commit to writing their life's final chapters with intention, respect, and love. The first step in creating a calm and mindful transition is to start with open conversations. We organize our physical world and strengthen the emotional bonds that give our existence meaning through these dialogues.

11.3.2. Organizing Important Documents

The practicality of Swedish death cleaning, or Döstädning, includes ensuring that the necessary paperwork is in order and decluttering physical items. Organizing important documents becomes essential in the context of end-of-life planning. Making sure that loved ones have all the information they need without having to search for it during a challenging time is more than just an act of organization; it's an expression of care.

Documents can significantly impact our lives, affecting everything from defining moments to leaving financial legacies. Our existence, our accomplishments, and our responsibilities are all documented by them. As a result, organizing them is crucial to the Döstädning journey to make them understandable and accessible. Begin by identifying what's essential. The list might include:

Will and testament: This document outlines your wishes regarding the division of your property and may also contain other crucial instructions.

Financial documents: Bank statements, insurance policies, tax returns, and asset and liability records provide a comprehensive picture of one's financial situation.

Medical records and directives: These documents clarify your medical history and wishes for medical decisions if you cannot make them.

Property deeds and titles: These papers establish ownership of everything from real estate to vehicles.

Personal documents: Birth certificates, marriage certificates, passports, and other identification documents.

Passwords and digital access: Ensuring access to online accounts, from social media to banking, is critical in today's digital age.

After identifying the critical documents, the next step is to securely store them. Consider purchasing a fireproof and waterproof safe or a bank-safe deposit box. These documents must remain intact and accessible. Make an inventory list of the contents of the safe or deposit box to serve as a guide for loved ones.

It is critical to update these documents regularly. Personal and financial circumstances both change. Regularly reviewing and updating this collection ensures that it remains reflective of your current state and wishes. Consider writing a concise guide or a letter to accompany these documents to further assist your loved ones. This guide can explain the significance or context of specific papers and provide a roadmap for any subsequent steps that must be taken.

Equally important is letting a trusted person, such as a member of the family, a lawyer, or a close friend, know where and how to access these documents. This act of trust guarantees that the required documents will be easily accessible at the appropriate time. Döstädning is a holistic philosophy, and organizing important documents is a demonstration of this. It involves weaving clarity into one's life's fabric and ensuring that everything—even the paperwork—is done with mindfulness, love, and intention.

By taking an organized approach, we give our loved ones a sense of security, which helps them cope with an already difficult time.

11.3.3.   Deciding on Heirlooms and Memorabilia

Memorabilia and heirlooms comprise a unique collection of possessions closely related to our family histories and personal stories. In contrast to everyday objects, these items frequently carry the weight of generations, tales from bygone eras, and cherished memories. Determining the fate of such treasures as we begin the Döstädning journey is a complex and emotional end goal.

Vintage jewelry passed down through the generations, old family photos, handwritten letters, and even family recipes can all be considered heirlooms. Their worth is frequently emotional rather than monetary. These items represent concrete representations of our ancestry, and choosing what to do with them is both meaningful and occasionally challenging.

Understanding the Significance

Introspection is the first step. It is essential to comprehend the significance of each heirloom in the family history and the tale behind it. Why has it survived for so many years? What emotion or history does it have? Exploring these tales can help make the next steps less confusing and overwhelming.

Dialogue with Loved Ones

Introspection is the first step. It is essential to comprehend the significance of each heirloom in the family history and the tale behind it. Why has it survived for so many years? What emotion or history does it have? Exploring these tales can help make the next steps less confusing and overwhelming.

Consideration of Practicality

The next generation may not keep every heirloom in their homes or lives. It's crucial to strike a balance between sentiment and reason. For instance, large furniture pieces might not fit into modern minimalist homes, and some jewelry might not be suitable for the tastes of the younger generation.

Preservation for the Future

Consider preserving certain items for future generations if they are significant but don't have immediate takers. Using appropriate storage methods can guarantee the preservation of textiles, papers, and other delicate items. Additionally, preserving the history and legend connected to each heirloom can give future generations context.

Gifting Outside the Family

Sometimes, no one in the family expresses interest in a specific heirloom. When this occurs, think about giving the item to museums or other organizations that can value and preserve it, especially if it has historical value. Giving it to close friends or other people who might value it is another option.

Transforming and Adapting

Sometimes, a new form can capture the essence of an heirloom. For instance, it is possible to incorporate material from a historical gown into a contemporary outfit or quilt. You can digitize or publish old letters as a book. Such modifications guarantee that the memory endures in a format better suited to modern lifestyles.

Some of the most emotional choices are made during the profound journey of Döstädning, thanks to heirlooms and memorabilia. We can ensure that the legacy they leave behind will be both significant and cherished by the generations that come after them by approaching them with understanding, respect, and an open dialogue. We honor the stories and memories they contain through this process, ensuring that they remain resonant in the tapestry of family history rather than just choosing the objects.

11.3.4. Addressing Items with Emotional Weight

There are items in our collections of personal possessions that go beyond simple utility. These items can arouse emotions, from joy and nostalgia to pain and sorrow, because they are loaded with memories, stories, and connections to important life events. When beginning the journey of Döstädning, decluttering these items calls for a delicate yet firm touch.

It's crucial to give oneself the time and space to experience and comprehend the emotions these emotionally charged objects elicit before making decisions about them. This might entail taking a moment to reflect, delving deeply into memories that you cherish, or facing up to past heartbreaks. Not only is the process about decluttering, but it also provides a way for emotional healing through acceptance and acknowledgment. Sharing an item's history is an effective way to comprehend and control the emotional significance of that item. Sharing can ease the emotional burden and provide a new perspective on the object by telling its history to a trusted friend or family member or journaling your feelings. If giving up the object seems difficult, consider preserving its essence in a memory journal. You can keep the memory alive without the physical object by taking a picture of it and writing a note or a story about what it means.

Letting go can be a powerful act. Consider performing a farewell ritual when it's time to say goodbye to an item with emotional significance. A quiet moment of gratitude or a more elaborate ceremony with loved ones can both be used to express gratitude. Such rituals are avenues to honor the memories tied to the item and find closure in its release. It's also important to recognize that this decluttering journey is not solo. Seeking advice from loved ones or experts can be extremely helpful when making decisions becomes especially difficult. Therapists, counselors, and decluttering professionals can all offer valuable insights and coping strategies.

Ultimately, the Döstädning process of dealing with items with emotional weight is transformative. Decluttering aims to achieve a deeper level of emotional clarity, peace, and renewal rather than just physical decluttering. To create a new story for the future, new physical and emotional spaces are created as items are let go. These spaces are ready to be filled with new experiences, memories, and emotions.

11.4. The Psychological Impact of Döstädning and End of Life Preparations

When combined with considerations about the end of one's life, the act of Döstädning can have significant psychological ramifications. It entails delving into the intricacies of one's emotional and psychological landscapes and letting go of objects from one's material possessions.

11.4.1: The Healing Power of Reflection and Letting Go

Especially when it overlaps with other end-of-life preparations, reflection is an essential component of the Döstädning process and serves as a cornerstone. One can access pleasant and difficult memories by revisiting previous experiences. In this context, releasing emotional baggage is analogous to letting go of physical items. There is a parallel process of healing old wounds, forgiving past mistakes, and celebrating cherished moments concurrently with discarding objects. Consequently, decluttering becomes a path to personal development, assisting individuals in achieving closure, finding peace, and revitalizing themselves.

11.4.2: Handling Grief and Nostalgia

Feelings of grief and nostalgia are unavoidable when sorting through items and memories. Due to their close connection to the transient nature of life, these emotions are a natural companion on the Döstädning journey. It is critical to acknowledge these feelings without judgment and give oneself the time and space to work through them. A person may experience grief due to past losses or the impending realization of their mortality. Nostalgia, on the other hand, can be a bittersweet reminder of times gone by. One can embrace these emotions, find solace in memories, and seek comfort in the knowledge that life, at its core, is a series of hellos and goodbyes when they participates in Döstädning.

11.4.3: Encouraging Family Involvement

Involving family members can help to share the emotional weight of Döstädning and, in many cases, lessen it. This creates an intergenerational dialogue wherein tales are told, knowledge is transmitted, and group memories are formed. Participation from the family ensures that the process is about coming together and letting go. It's a chance for elders to share wisdom and values and for younger generations to learn about their heritage. A valuable space for group healing and growth, this shared experience can fortify family bonds and support one another.

While Döstädning involves preparing for the end of life, its psychological effects are far-reaching and impact every aspect of an individual's life. It's a testament to the beauty of introspection, connection, and development, as well as a reminder of the transience of life. One gains psychological clarity, emotional peace, and a fresh sense of purpose through this process, in addition to clearing out physical spaces.

11.5. Overcoming Challenges in the Process

Döstädning is a challenging journey, especially when planning for the end of one's life. These challenges are profoundly emotional and psychological rather than merely being of a physical or logistical nature. To have a meaningful and healing experience, it is crucial to approach them with consideration, patience, and understanding.

11.6. Seeking Professional Guidance: Therapists and Organizers

Döstädning is a process that can be extremely rewarding; however, it can also be a demanding process that could benefit from the intervention and invaluable support of professionals. Experts can provide substantial support, whether it be helping someone navigate the emotional labyrinth or ensuring that the decluttering process is efficient and effective.

11.6.1. Balancing Emotional Well-being with Practical Decisions

Finding a balance between one's emotional health and pragmatic choices can be intricate. Therapists, especially those who focus on grief or geriatric care, can provide coping mechanisms, emotional support, and strategies to deal with the complex emotions that come up during Döstädning. On the other hand, professional organizers can make sure that the decluttering process is consistent with the client's emotional journey. They bring a structured approach that makes the procedure effective, manageable, and less overwhelming. Combining the skills of the two professionals ensures a balanced approach to Döstädning that addresses both the heart and the home.

11.7. Legacy Building and Döstädning

Legacy includes the values, memories, wisdom, and tales that characterize our life journey through belongings and the tangible items we leave behind. We are given the unique opportunity as we journey into the profound depths of Döstädning to purge our possessions and thoughtfully curate what we want to leave behind for future generations. This chapter explores the interconnected worlds of legacy creation and Döstädning, highlighting the significance of transmitting possessions and a sense of direction and passion to future generations. We'll look at how to ensure that our legacy includes our belongings and the essence of who we are through a compassionate approach.

11.7.1. Defining One's Legacy

Every person, whether intentionally or not, leaves behind a legacy. It is a tapestry made of the threads of our deeds, convictions, successes, connections, and the love we have both given and received. Döstädning, on the other hand, forces us to confront and carefully choose what we want to leave behind by making thinking about our legacy an intentional act. Material possessions are only one aspect of legacy. The true meaning of a person's legacy is found in the intangible—the lessons we've taught, the love we've spread, and the wisdom we've gained—rather than in heirlooms and memorabilia.

Some people can see their legacy in the works of art, books, or community projects they have contributed to. Others find it encapsulated in the morals they've taught their kids, the tales they've told, or the small deeds of kindness they've performed throughout their lives.

Defining one's legacy requires deep introspection.

It's very important to:

❖ Reflect on life's pivotal moments and the lessons learned from them.

❖ Contemplate the principles that have served as your compass and how you want the world to continue to be shaped by these values and beliefs after you are gone.

❖ Recognize and honor the relationships and connections that have improved your life. What impact have they had on others, and how do they want to be remembered by them?

❖ Consider the positive contributions made to the community or the world, whether large or small. Every act, from planting a tree to mentoring someone, contributes to one's legacy.

We can ensure that Döstädning becomes a process that not only declutters our physical space but also clarifies the mark we want to leave on the world by understanding and articulating our legacy. It becomes a mindful act of preparing for the end of life and the continuation of our spirit and essence in the stories, values, and memories we pass down to the next generation.

11.7.2. Ensuring Memories and Values Live On

Each experience, relationship, and challenge on our life's journey adds layers to our personal narrative. These stories, values, and memories shape who we are and the legacy we leave behind. Döstädning is more than just the tangible items we leave behind; it is also about how we ensure the essence of who we are and what we believe in lives on in the hearts and minds of those we love.

Our values form the foundation of our personality. They serve as guiding principles, influencing our decisions, behaviors, and interactions. These values are frequently passed down through generations, either explicitly via lessons and conversations or implicitly via observed behaviors and family traditions.

Some points to remember:

Conversations with Loved Ones: An open dialogue is essential. Sharing stories from our past, lessons learned, challenges overcome, and happy and sad moments helps our loved ones understand our journey and the values that guided us. These personal anecdotes frequently leave a stronger impression than any written document.

Documenting Your Journey: There are numerous ways to document one's life journey in the digital age. Making digital albums, recording audio memories, or writing an autobiography or memoir are all effective ways to record moments and lessons. These documents become treasured possessions for loved ones, providing information about their ancestors and lineage.

Family Rituals and Traditions: Traditions have a way of passing down values to succeeding generations. Whether it's a yearly family gathering, a particular holiday custom, or even a simple Sunday family dinner, these traditions are filled with memories, lessons, and values. They serve as pillars, a constant reminder of the family's history and core values.

Teaching by Example: Values are best transmitted through deeds rather than words. Kindness, integrity, perseverance, or any other value demonstrated daily leaves a lasting impression on family members. Since our actions teach those around us valuable real-life lessons, it is crucial to be mindful of them.

Creating Legacy Projects: One's values and passions are embodied in these initiatives or projects. It might be a family cookbook, a community garden, or a scholarship fund. Through such endeavors, one can ensure that one's values and passions influence and benefit others for years.

It takes intentionality to ensure that memories and values endure the test of time. By engaging in Döstädning, we are paving the way for our essence to continue influencing, guiding, and guiding future generations and clearing our physical spaces. It's a lovely testament to how, even though life is short, the impact of our stories and values can last forever.

11.7.3. Sharing Stories and Wisdom with Future Generations

Sharing knowledge and wisdom holds a significant place in the meticulous practice of Döstädning, acting as the intangible legacy left to succeeding generations. The richness of a well-lived life is communicated through the sharing of tales, anecdotes, life lessons, and insights, transcending the transient nature of physical existence and transforming it into an everlasting reservoir of knowledge and wisdom.

Every family has its own set of legendary tales and anecdotes that perfectly capture the character of a member of the values of the whole unit. A platform for sharing experiences, moral lessons, and reflections is provided by oral narration. The interaction between generations enables the younger generation to learn from and be inspired by the experiences of their forebears. Writing also plays a crucial part. People create a tangible repository of their journey, thought processes, and philosophies by writing letters, memoirs, or even compiling a collection of pivotal moments from their lives. This written legacy serves as a lighthouse, illuminating the way for coming generations and providing advice, comfort, and a strong sense of connection.

Facilitating conversation, debate, and reflection on the many facets of life fosters a culture of learning and mutual development. Knowledge, principles, and values are transmitted through this open discussion, which fosters a profound appreciation for shared generational wisdom. It is also pivotal to clearly define the fundamental values, tenets, and moral guidelines that have guided one's life journey. Incorporating these values into family discussions, lessons, and regular interactions makes them intricately woven into the family unit and influences subsequent generations' sense of morality.

With the advent of technology, capturing one's journey, wisdom, and insights through videos or audio recordings has become a powerful tool. Future generations can form a deeply personal and immersive connection with their ancestors by hearing their voices, seeing their expressions, and experiencing their emotions through these multimedia artifacts. Additionally, it fosters a strong sense of identity and belonging when family members are encouraged to consider and internalize the shared stories, values, and lessons. By reflecting on their heritage, they can develop a deeper understanding of it, allowing the wisdom and lessons of the past to influence their present and shape their future.

Embracing Döstädning guides people on a reflective journey to determine their legacies. This process is a holistic way of preserving one's essence; it goes beyond simple decluttering. By ensuring that the tapestry of stories, wisdom, and values continues to inspire, guide, and warm the hearts of generations yet unborn, the transient journey of life becomes an eternal odyssey of learning and love.

Conclusion: Looking Forward with Clarity and Purpose

What an enlightening journey we've shared, diving into the heart of Swedish Death Cleaning, or Döstädning! Döstädning's essence is a gentle reminder of life's ever-changing dance, nudging us to embrace each moment, cherish every memory, and eagerly await the wonders yet to come. It's not just about cleaning; it's an invitation to celebrate life in all its vibrant hues, to deepen our connections, and to approach each day with vigor.

This Swedish gem teaches us that an abundance of life's joys is waiting to be rediscovered in the simplicity of decluttering. We've uncovered the beautiful mosaic of our lives by removing the unnecessary, allowing our most cherished memories, dreams, and aspirations to shine even brighter.

Let us sprinkle Döstädning's magic into every corner of our lives. By encouraging this joyful and mindful approach, we create an atmosphere in which gratitude thrives, every moment becomes a gift, and every day is a blank canvas of possibilities. This journey has equipped us with home organization strategies and the delightful mindset of welcoming life's blessings with open arms.

Let us keep this newfound clarity close to our hearts as we move into tomorrow, illuminating our paths with joy and purpose. The words in this book have painted a beautiful picture: with Döstädning every day becomes a celebration, every memory a treasure, and every moment an opportunity to live with clarity and purpose. Cheers to a bright future packed with joy and happiness!

Frederick

Printed in Great Britain
by Amazon

44521286R00057